Praise for *Say It*

"This isn't just a book on self-talk. *Say It O[...]* [...] mission slip we all need to start talking t[...] [...] our head, rather than being influenced by all of those around us."

— **Ajit Nawalkha**, cofounder of Evercoach and author of *Live Big*

"I know the brilliance of Vasavi Kumar firsthand. This book is sure to ignite a new energy within you and your ability to clearly claim the life of your dreams."

— **Alyson Charles**, bestselling author of *Animal Power* and host of the internationally acclaimed *Ceremony Circle* podcast

"*Say It Out Loud* is a game changer! Vasavi Kumar shows you how to use the power of your own voice to courageously pursue your dreams. With Vasavi's fun and focused guidance, you'll discover that your voice really does have the power to create a better life."

— **Izabella Wentz**, PharmD,
New York Times bestselling author of *Hashimoto's Protocol*

"The future belongs to the brave, and Vasavi Kumar lights the way in her bold, fun, courageous personal development debut."

— **Judi Holler**, bestselling author of *Fear Is My Homeboy*
and founder of the Disco Ball Project™

"*Say It Out Loud* is so original! The fundamental idea that saying something out loud alone has power is totally new to me, and from practicing, I can already see how impactful it can be. Vasavi Kumar has been through so much, and she hasn't wasted it, because she's got wisdom up the wazoo. What she suggests in this book will probably make you uncomfortable, as it did me, and that's a really good thing."

— **Kate Northrup**, bestselling author of *Do Less*

"Saying it out loud is transformational and vital for reaching your next level in life. Read, reread, and then read it again! Your time is now."

— **Dr. Kerrie Carter-Walker**, serial entrepreneur
(realtor, investor, transformational speaker, and coach)

"There are plenty of books on how to tap into the source of your creativity, but *Say It Out Loud* gets to the root of what blocks our true creative potential from being fulfilled. Vasavi Kumar has lived through her own personal trials and tribulations and fully understands the specific challenges that every human being faces when it comes to speaking to ourselves with love and respect. This book is a must-have on your nightstand, reminding you to share your truth unapologetically as Vasavi, so raw and real, does in this book."
— **Dr. Neeta Bhushan**, author of *That Sucked. Now What?* and host of *The Brave Table* podcast

"*Say It Out Loud* is a beautiful invitation to learn the language of ourselves. The book spoke to me deeply, and I couldn't put it down. Vasavi Kumar's transparency is refreshing, and her fiery support and tested tools are the guide we need to speak our deepest fears, needs, and desires out into the world. The powerful exercises in *Say It Out Loud* will challenge you — and they're meant to. On the other side of this narrative shift and emotional unearthing are the transformation and joy you deserve. It's time to turn up the volume on your life — and this book will get you there."
— **Richelle Fredson**, book publishing coach and host of *Bound + Determined* podcast

"Vasavi Kumar is a powerful voice for women who are ready to reclaim their power."
— **Selena Soo**, creator of Impacting Millions

"*Say It Out Loud* is a masterclass that teaches you how to offer compassion, creativity, and acceptance to your painful inner narratives."
— **Silvy Khoucasian**, MA, relationship expert and writer

SAY IT
OUT
LOUD

SAY IT OUT LOUD

USING the POWER of YOUR VOICE
to LISTEN to YOUR DEEPEST
THOUGHTS and COURAGEOUSLY
PURSUE YOUR DREAMS

VASAVI KUMAR

Foreword by Lisa Nichols

New World Library
Novato, California

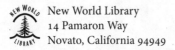 New World Library
14 Pamaron Way
Novato, California 94949

The material in this book is intended for education. No expressed or implied guarantee of the effects of the use of the recommendations can be given or liability taken. The author's experiences used as examples throughout this book are true, although identifying details such as names and locations have been changed to protect privacy.

Text design by Tona Pearce Myers

Library of Congress Cataloging-in-Publication data is available.

First printing, May 2023
ISBN 978-1-60868-826-5
Ebook ISBN 978-1-60868-827-2
Printed in Canada on 100% postconsumer-waste recycled paper

 New World Library is proud to be a Gold Certified Environmentally Responsible Publisher. Publisher certification awarded by Green Press Initiative.

10   9   8   7   6   5   4   3   2   1

To all those who suffer in silence:
may this book bring you relief.

CONTENTS

FOREWORD

In 2011, a young Indian American woman by the name of Vasavi Kumar enrolled in my yearlong Global Leadership Program. She was full of life, was hungry to learn, and was a breath of fresh air.

Vasavi wanted to make sense out of everything she had gone through in her life. One of the things she was most scared of sharing with others was her bipolar disorder diagnosis. She was terrified that the Indian community would judge her and that no one would take her seriously as a female business owner. The first time she shared her mental health journey with the rest of her colleagues and me, I remember thinking, "This young girl has a brilliant brain and will change lives." No matter how uncomfortable in her skin she felt while I coached her through her stories, beliefs, and perceptions of herself, she would soak in every word and nod her head yes. She was hungry to find her truth and was willing to do whatever it took to know every single part of herself.

As her coach and mentor, I have watched her blossom into

a woman who stands for honesty no matter what. As an author, speaker, and coach, I know the depth of internal reprogramming that needed to take place for Vasavi to have written a book called *Say It Out Loud*. In order to write this book, she has had to fight and work through her own inner demons while offering grace and acceptance toward herself and others.

Say It Out Loud is the antidote to the parts of ourselves that still suffer in silence. If you have picked up this book in the hopes of reconnecting with your inner voices and different parts of yourself, I have no doubt that it will change your life. Trust that you have been divinely guided to reach for this volume because some part of you chose it. Honor what you've been through and how you got *here*. Give voice to the parts of you that have yet to speak. Read every line of this book; let them soak in. Your voice needs to be heard. It's time for you to say it out loud.

In love and transformation,
Lisa Nichols
New York Times bestselling author of *Abundance Now*

INTRODUCTION

Let me be the first to say that me writing a book titled *Say It Out Loud* is proof that you have the power to create anything you want, when you learn how to talk to yourself. You see, when I was a kid, I talked. A lot. My mother would half-jokingly say to me, "Vasavi, *chuma ire*," which loosely translates in our native language of Tamil as "Vasavi, stop talking." So it's kind of ironic for me to be writing a book called *Say It Out Loud*, don't you think? The very thing I got in trouble for as a kid (my outspoken nature) is now the foundation of my work: helping other people use their voice to courageously pursue their dreams. Imagine if I had taken "*chuma ire*" to heart and listened to my mother (which I rarely did) — I wouldn't be where I am today. Instead, I've spent my life working on the most important relationship I have: the one with the voices in my head.

When I was young, I would stand in between my parents during one of their many squabbles and mediate between them. "OK," I'd say to one of them, "you say how you feel out loud," and then I would turn to my other parent and direct, "OK, now *you* listen, and then you say how you really feel out loud." Watching them was like witnessing two children hungry for understanding and attention. I could sense my mother's frustration and would say to my dad, "Why are you ignoring her? She's talking to you!" and I would say to my mother, "Please stop yelling. It's just making things worse." When I sensed that neither one of them was saying how they felt, I spoke up for them. I learned how to navigate the tension in the room by calling out the obvious. That is how I taught myself to cope amid chaos. I said it out loud, even though I should have probably just "*chuma ire*."

Of course, looking back now, having been married, divorced, and in a series of unhealthy friendships and relationships, I can clearly understand how difficult it was for my parents, who didn't know how to communicate their truest feelings to each other. At my very core, I didn't want to end up like my parents, but in a way I already had. I had absorbed all of *their* unsaid feelings. The truth is, I didn't know where they ended and I began.

At an early age, we are extraordinarily sensitive, impressionable, and pure; we are like sponges soaking up all the verbal and nonverbal cues that are directed at us. The voices in my head I've had to battle throughout my life belonged to none other than my mother, my father, and my very sad inner child. It made complete sense that I struggled as an adult to say it out loud to the people in my life. As I got older and entered friendships and romantic relationships, what had started out as just the voices of my parents and my inner child grew to include voices of failed friendships and romantic relationships — voices that said things like, "It's safer to be alone," or "All men are dogs," or, in my professional life, "You should be farther along by now," or "You're not smart enough." At some point, we have to stop and ask ourselves out loud, "Whose voice is this?" The truth of who you are has been drowned out by the voices of everyone else in your life.

It's time to clear out the voices in your head that do not belong to you *and never did*.

As the adage goes, "We teach what we need to learn." I went on to get a master's degree in special education and one in social work, with the hopes of equipping myself with the tools to help people make sense out of their own lives. However, in my personal life, I often picked romantic partners who were emotionally unavailable and triggered my most sensitive childhood wounds, recreating the dysfunctional dynamic I had witnessed between my parents. While I knew exactly how to support others in the regulation of their emotions, I struggled with taking my own advice. I know now I was trying to heal my traumas by recreating them in my romantic partnerships. I could spot the red flags from a mile away but would often ignore them and feel even more attracted to my partners because of them. I often stayed in toxic relationships much longer than necessary, and I thrived in the face of chaos — just like when I was standing in between my parents and playing the role of mediator. Yet I was able to turn my unsuccessful attempts to foster communication and healing between my parents into a purposeful career. In my professional life I continued to play the role of mediator, healer, therapist, and coach with my clients, but to a more effective and healing end.

Over the last decade, I have been given many opportunities to bring together the parts of myself that split off from me through the various experiences in my life: being a first-generation Indian immigrant growing up in a predominately all-white town; being subjected to emotional and psychological abuse in my early years; undergoing sexual trauma in my young adult years; being diagnosed with bipolar disorder; and going through marriage, divorce, addiction, and recovery. I finally came back home to myself while learning how to sit through discomfort, to embrace my most painful emotions, and to talk to myself throughout it all. All of these experiences set the foundation for what I would create many years later: this book; my podcast, *Say It Out Loud with Vasavi*; and the Say It Out Loud community for creatives, entrepreneurs, and business owners, my online support group where every single person is committed to learning how to master their self-talk, honored for being exactly who they are, and celebrated for who they want to become. Many of the stories that I share throughout this book come from me not knowing any better — correction: from me not trusting myself when I *did* know better. I share them out loud with you because I know that in reading my stories, and the stories of my clients, you'll see that you're not alone in feeling and thinking the way you do. And maybe you'll be inspired to be more authentically you and start to trust that it is safe for *you* to say it out loud.

Rather than being concerned with how others are going to perceive you or fearing that they will see right through you, you'll start owning every single part of you — the good, the bad, and the ugly. Your shame shrivels and your confidence expands when you're being exactly who you want to be, not who you think you should be. When you own and speak the darkest parts of yourself out loud, people's opinions of you no longer control you, because you've delved into every single part of you and know yourself through and through. When you own your stuff, what can anyone possibly say about you? Sure, they might not like you; they might say things about you behind your back or even to your face. But when you own who you are and are the embodiment of your truth, you become one with yourself. And as a result of owning every part of you, the next time you go to a social gathering or get ready for a job interview, you're not concerned with saying and doing the "right" thing; instead, you are clear and confident in who you are, exactly as you are.

How you talk to yourself matters. It sets the tone for every experience in your life. It will bring you either closer to or farther from the truth of who you are. Whether you take the time to speak words of tenderness and care to yourself or use a cold, dismissive tone of voice, how you've been speaking to yourself has gotten you up to this point. Deep inside, you know that parts of you have been suppressed for far too long. You are starting to or have already awakened to the fact that not speaking up for yourself is costing you your mental and emotional well-being. There is power in saying our thoughts out loud. It allows us to step back and ask ourselves, "Is the way that I'm speaking to myself helpful or hurtful?"

The practice of talking to yourself, especially out loud, is a vulnerable and sacred act of communion. Your deepest thoughts and feelings, the ones that you have never shared with anyone, are *yours*. No matter how close anyone is to you, there are parts of you that *only you know*. Saying your thoughts and feelings out loud is transforming their sanctity into actual spoken words. When you practice rigorous honesty with yourself and get comfortable saying your thoughts out loud, you will no longer hold back on authentically communicating with everyone in your life. Things that normally would throw you onto an emotional roller coaster will no longer be able to decenter you, because you feel safe in your own skin to be and speak your truth.

I was inspired by my own recovery journey when I designed the outline for this book. Having gone through the 12-step programs of Alcoholics Anonymous and Narcotics Anonymous, I decided to create my own version for you. However, this isn't *just* a step-by-step self-talk instructional manual. It's a reminder to be mindful and intentional with the words that you use when speaking to yourself. It's about giving yourself permission to pause and reflect on what's going on in the present moment, to turn your awareness inward to observe your responses, reactions, and judgments and make sense of what's going on inside, rather than turning outward toward distractions, addictive substances, or toxic relationships to soothe you. In a nutshell, this book will teach you how to reconnect with the lost parts of yourself by engaging in a curious, compassionate dialogue with these parts, out loud, and tapping into your Higher Self — the wise knower that lives within you. My mission is to help you express your deepest thoughts out loud, create a rock-solid relationship with yourself, and facilitate the courageous pursuit of a fulfilling life. You will learn how to question your thoughts with curiosity and kindness. You will have fun finding out the type of tone, volume, and inflection to which you best respond. You will become your safest confidante both in times of need and in moments of celebration.

The concepts in this book will teach you how to talk to all the parts of yourself. When you learn to acknowledge every single part that exists inside you, practice being honest with how you really feel, and say your deepest thoughts out loud, you release all the things that have been emotionally clogging you up. And when you become a clear channel for your creative spirit to move through you, your dreams suddenly seem reachable.

My promise to you is this: when you learn how to talk to yourself and give a voice to every single part of you, you won't hem and haw over what to say or how to say it; instead, you will be direct and confident in your communication. We meet people with as much depth and connection as we are willing to have within ourselves. You'll learn how to uncomplicate seemingly complicated challenges, all because you have become your own voice of encouragement and reason. You'll learn how to think for yourself rather than constantly ask for feedback. You'll learn how to connect with the wisdom of your body, develop your intuition, and make values-based decisions. You'll begin to trust that something bigger than yourself (I reference God throughout the book; please use whatever word feels best to you) truly has been guiding you from day one of your existence and even before you were brought into this physical form.

In chapter 1, you'll see that there are specific ways to talk to yourself out loud to help you move through any resistance, obstacles, and heavy emotions. You will start to notice how you typically speak to yourself. In chapter 2, we will begin to move you toward saying it out loud by identifying the areas where you feel powerless. This takes an immense amount of honesty with yourself. When you admit where you feel powerless, then you can really start to notice the triggers that make you believe you *are* powerless. Your triggers provide you with information to help you understand the underlying beliefs that run your life. And in chapter 3, you will discover how to talk to your triggers out loud.

The culmination of all your beliefs are the stories of your life, and many of us have been operating as a character in a story. In chapter 4 you will take the time to transform your story by asking yourself out loud, "Is this the story that I want to keep living?" Waking up to the reality that your life has been shaped by beliefs and stories that have held you back will bring up many emotions, which is why, in chapter 5, you will give yourself permission to express your feelings out loud. In chapter 6, you'll start to become more in touch with your intuition, the soft whisper that we tend to ignore. Now that you're getting in the habit of saying your truth out loud, the voice of your intuition will become easier to access.

But be prepared: when you begin to listen to your intuition rather than all the old voices of doubt, resistance inevitably creeps up. It is totally normal to be confronted with that voice that tells you you're crazy for trusting the soft whisper inside you. In chapter 7, I will teach you the power of gentle firmness when voicing your resistance out loud. You will no longer be controlled by your resistance; instead, you will become the voice of motivation and encouragement that you need to keep you going when times get tough (which they will). In chapter 8, I will reveal the secret to being the most confident person you know: owning your flaws out loud. When you learn to own your flaws out loud, you become an open book with nothing to hide.

This book is about bringing *all* the parts of you together, and that includes the parts that you've kept hidden. Plan on having fun with chapter 9, as you continue to create a safe space to play hide-and-seek with the parts of yourself that you've tucked away. At this point in the book, you're becoming even more real and honest with yourself. You're calling out your dark side, holding the mirror up to yourself, and giving each part of you a voice to express itself out loud. Your job is to be curious about each part of you. That's inner freedom, my friend. And when you have inner freedom, you can make clear decisions that are aligned with your true desires. You are no longer held back by the opinions of others because you know yourself inside and out and have nothing to hide. Rather than putting on a show for others, you are starting to live a life that is authentically you.

It's time to reframe how we look at prioritizing ourselves. Chapter 10 will help you work through any feelings of selfishness and guilt that might emerge as you continue to become more of who you really are and prioritize your needs, wants, and desires. I want you to unashamedly claim the life that you want, which requires you to choose yourself first, every time. In chapter 11, you're going to practice voicing your desires and decisions out loud. I'm training you to become a person with full faith and confidence in your decision-making abilities, someone who is crystal clear about his or her worthiness, able to ask for and receive all that life has to offer. Lastly, in chapter 12, you will learn that it is safe to live your life out loud. You can be all of you and still be loved for exactly who you are. I am proof of that, and I want you to *access the inner freedom and peace that are already within you.* They are yours. You are the one you have been searching for.

At the end of every chapter, you will be guided through a Say It Out Loud exercise. The simple exercise at the end of chapter 1 is meant to open up your awareness about how you currently talk to yourself. Beginning with chapter 2, each exercise consists of a prompt, practice, and promise. I designed these exercises to help you start using your voice with yourself. Every prompt is intended to expand your awareness: to help you start noticing how you speak to yourself, how you react to situations, and what you tell yourself about how you "should" and "shouldn't" be. The practices help you learn how to talk to yourself using questions that are rooted in curiosity, rather than confrontation. The promises are commitments to yourself to be more understanding, compassionate, and, at times when you need it, firm with yourself. I'll also give you a set of accompanying affirmations to say out loud as you move through each chapter. Feel free to write these affirmations on sticky notes and place them throughout your house. Every time you walk past one, *say it out loud.* Or, if you want to take it a step further, record yourself saying each of these affirmations out loud and play them back to yourself every time you need a dose of encouragement.

Remember, talking to yourself out loud is a process that goes beyond this book: it is a lifelong practice. Years into it, just when you think you've uncovered all your stories, another one may pop up. And that's OK, because you will have learned how to talk to yourself through it, by being curious and compassionate with yourself. The goal of this book is to help you start using your voice as the sacred instrument that it is, an instrument that will guide you to your next step and the next step after that. Because your voice is that powerful.

I am grateful to be alive another day to share with you what I have learned throughout my life. Trust the power of your voice. Trust that your deepest thoughts and feelings are inside you to be manifested in physical form through creative self-expression. With time, energy, pure presence, and attention inward, you will be, do, and create anything you desire. Thank you for picking up this book and for giving yourself permission to be the type of person who speaks their truth, no matter what. You're about to embark on the most fun, expansive, and exhilarating ride of your life.

Chapter 1

SAY YOUR THOUGHTS
OUT LOUD

Answer this out loud:
Do you think it's weird to talk to yourself out loud?

Is there any part of you that thinks it's weird to talk to yourself out loud? If you answered yes, I want to celebrate you for exploring an idea that makes you uncomfortable. If you answered no, then welcome! You're in the right place. And if you're on the fence, stay curious and open. In this chapter, you're going to learn different ways of talking to yourself, plus the mechanics of *how* to talk to yourself, which is foundational to receiving the benefits of the Say It Out Loud exercises at the end of each chapter.

From early childhood, our inner dialogue (also sometimes referred to as self-talk or thinking to yourself) plays an essential role in how we think, feel, and act. And while you may be the type of person who keeps your inner dialogues hidden (except for a few mortifying moments here and there), what you're telling yourself and how you're speaking to yourself internally are far more important than you realize. Think about how many times you've prepared to have a difficult conversation with your boss, friend, partner, or family member. Rehearsing what you want to say, predicting what they might say — all this helped you to prepare for the possible best-case and worst-case outcomes, didn't it? You internally played out every potential scenario to guard you against any surprising attacks from the other person. You went in equipped with the perfect strategy to avoid as much pain as you could. Your inner dialogue can be your greatest ally when getting ready for difficult conversations and other stressful situations.

Your inner dialogue can also be your biggest hater. As human beings, we cannot help but judge everything and everyone around us. Raise your hand if you love people watching! It's entertaining to observe people and make up scenarios and stories about their lives. We create stories in our head about the people we see while scrolling through Instagram, or when a friend doesn't invite us to their birthday party, or when we're on the receiving end of a cashier's bad day at the grocery store. And while this may seem harmless and even feel like fun and games sometimes, think about when you turn that inner dialogue against yourself — for example, when you compare yourself to that influencer you saw on Instagram and tell yourself that your life isn't as fabulous as theirs and you clearly are falling behind, or you tell yourself that you're unlucky and good things just don't happen to you. The truth is, the stories and judgments that you have about *yourself* can be detrimental to your mental and emotional health, making it difficult to even take the first step toward courageously pursuing your dreams.

Why would you drown yourself in criticism and cruelty? All I'm saying is, be kind to yourself. Stop judging your every move. In the moments of quiet when you notice your thoughts are beating you up, practice saying them out loud so you can respond with love. Remember, you're learning how to talk to yourself. You're replacing the mean thoughts with loving ones, through your spoken words. And once you find your authentic way of speaking to yourself, your so-called judgments will stop feeling so *judgy*, and you will sharpen your discernment regarding what you want and what you don't want in your life. For example, rather than saying to yourself, "I'm so bad with money," when you learn how to speak to yourself, the conversation might sound like, "I'm smart and savvy enough to figure out my finances." *Boom!* You go from being someone who is "bad with money" to someone who is "smart and savvy." From there you focus on seeking solutions, rather than shaming yourself. Way more helpful, don't you think? If you're going to judge yourself, judge with the intention of understanding yourself. Start understanding yourself, and you'll stop being so scared of other people judging you.

Being clear and honest with others is the foundation for healthy and fulfilling relationships. The way you communicate with others is a direct reflection of how you communicate with yourself. The thoughts you think, which are nothing more than words guiding you daily, will directly impact how you speak to others. So it follows that when you learn how to talk to yourself with kindness, respect, and compassion, you will be able to extend that to others. This does not mean you put up with people overstepping your boundaries. In fact, quite the opposite. When you talk to yourself with respect, you will no longer tolerate mistreatment from others, and you will be able to state your boundaries out loud.

You're not crazy for talking *and responding* to yourself out loud.

When I returned to playing tennis a few years ago, one thing became abundantly evident to me: how I spoke to myself on the court (both out loud and internally) had a direct impact on my performance. Whether we're playing a sport or attempting to practice a new musical instrument or read a book, our inner speech will either psych us up or convince us to throw in the towel and walk away. Our self-talk affects everything from our emotional control to our management of stress, anxiety, and depression. The right inner dialogue not only helps us overcome self-doubt and fear of failure, but it also helps us stay motivated.

The voices in your head that seem to have a nonstop commentary about every little thing you do, see, feel, think, and experience shape your entire reality. Often, we get stuck in a never-ending downward spiral of thoughts and "what if" scenarios. Running these kinds of thoughts through your head keeps the chaos alive. Actively asking and responding to questions out loud can help turn your jumble of thoughts into a more organized system.

And if you still need a bit of persuading that you're not crazy for talking to yourself out loud, here it is. Have you ever seen a small child talking to themselves while performing a task? Whether they're learning to tie their shoelaces, role-playing characters, or working through a difficult task, children naturally speak their thoughts out loud as they begin to explore the world around them and develop language. The question then becomes, At what point did our outer speech become inner speech as we got older? If as children we would talk out loud to ourselves to direct our behavior, when did we stop saying it out loud? Most likely when we first encountered condemnation for speaking the truth.

That's the irony. We're told to tell the truth and then punished when we do. Whether love was withheld or we were met with disapproval for speaking our minds, the underlying message was, "Tell the truth, but not too much of it, because if you do, you might upset someone." Or "Don't act like you're disappointed, because then you might make someone feel bad." We continue to tell white lies to others, and even bigger ones to ourselves, all so we can ensure that people won't feel bad or abandon us. If our out-loud speech — the purest form of creation — guided our intellect and behavior as children, wouldn't it make sense that saying it out loud as adults leads to courageously pursuing our dreams? There's one way to find out: #sayitoutloud.

> **It's not just what you say; it's how you say it.**

The approach I use to speak to myself has softened tremendously throughout the course of my life. Growing up in a first-generation Indian immigrant home, I was terrified of my mother. She could simply say, "Vasavi, *inga va*," which translates to "Vasavi, come here," and my heart would beat faster. Her tone of voice jolted my nervous system. As an adult, I respect her directness. She doesn't sugarcoat anything. But my nervous system didn't quite get that as a young child. And I'm mindful today of the fact that if I use a harsh or loud tone with my inner child, she will curl up in the fetal position. This is why I'm encouraging you to speak out loud. You cannot run from the harshness of your own tone that you use with yourself when you say it out loud. My hope is that when you hear how you're speaking to yourself, you will choose a kinder approach as an act of self-respect.

Our internal monologue communicates with us throughout the day; for some people, it goes nonstop. Whether you've been aware of your inner voice or you're now waking up to the dialogue that has been running in the background of your mind, there are small shifts you can make in the language you use to communicate with yourself, which can influence your ability to regulate your thoughts, emotions, and behavior in stressful situations. It's not just the ability to talk to yourself that has an impact, but the nuances of communicating, such as tone, volume, playfulness, and using our first name in self-talk. The tone you use with yourself affects how you feel in your own presence. If the way you speak to yourself has a harsh and unkind tone, then of course you're going to feel attacked by your own mind. Do you speak loudly to yourself to get motivated? Has it been working for you? Maybe it's time to use a softer volume. Or have you noticed that when you're lighter and sillier with yourself, you actually manage to move through challenges a lot more easily? Using a more playful approach with yourself might just be the key to moving through your fears. Do you use harsh words to motivate yourself? Using your first name might be more effective and less damaging to your psyche. There's no "right" way to say it out loud, but there are guidelines that will make this process enjoyable and open your heart back up to yourself.

Get curious about different approaches in tone, volume, playfulness, and how you address yourself. Tone, for example, is a subtle but powerful element of self-talk that will drastically improve how you feel about yourself if you shift it. Pay attention to different types of tones that resonate with you and notice those that trigger you. For example, I used to get really turned off by people who spoke with little emotion. I would freeze in the moment and immediately think that I had done something wrong, like I was back in school. I would ask myself out loud, "How does this tone of voice make me feel about myself?" And then the truth would emerge, which I would also say out loud: "I feel like I've been a bad girl and I'm in trouble and being sent to the principal's office."

By talking to myself out loud (usually in the privacy of my car or in front of the mirror), I was able to understand which part of me was easily upset with this tone of voice. I took the time to pay attention to what was underneath the surface of what seemed like just a mild fear of a specific tone. I was able to talk nurturingly to the part of myself that always felt like she was in trouble if someone used "that" tone of voice. Now, when I do talk to people and encounter that same tone that used to get me all frazzled, I soothe myself internally by saying, "Vasavi, don't take it personally. You're not in trouble." And I made a promise not to talk to myself in this way.

Take the time to understand which styles of communication work for you. Start experimenting with different ranges of tone, inflection, volume, and speed. The volume that I use with myself varies from situation to situation. When I need to focus, I will speak to myself calmly and with a low volume: "Come on, Vas, time to focus." When I need to pump myself up before a podcast interview or a social gathering, I will increase my volume and energy: "We're going to have the best time, Vasavi!!!" I am my biggest cheerleader.

> **Speak to yourself the way you want to be spoken to.**

Pay attention to the people in your life with whom you feel safe. For example, my friend Silvy uses a soft tone and volume when speaking to me. At first, it was a new style of communication that I hadn't experienced, even with myself. But the more time I spent with Silvy, the more I was drawn to her tone and volume, and now, I use that same gentle tone and volume with myself! Being around her taught me to be kinder and more nurturing toward myself.

My other friend, Neeta, is one of the calmest human beings

to be around. I playfully call her the Queen of Composed Confidence. Whenever I come to her with something stressful, she has a way of speaking and acknowledging what I'm going through that doesn't add fuel to my fire. I instantly feel more calm and grounded after speaking to her. Now, when I'm stressed out about things that I have no control over, I practice speaking to myself in a calm and composed way, the way Neeta would. You already have examples of people in your life who can show you exactly what types of communication you are drawn to or are repelled by. Start using interactions with others as information to help you better communicate with yourself.

At the end of the day, what you say, and how you say it to yourself, matters. Stay open to using new approaches as you're learning to talk to yourself. At times you may be going through something and in that moment what you need is a playful approach to loosen up your energy, which may sound like, "All right, honeybuns, we can do this, let's go!" Or you might need a firmer approach in a situation when you're up against your procrastination habit; then you might say to yourself out loud, "I know you don't want to sit down and do this, but you're on a deadline, so we've gotta focus," because what you need in that moment is structure and devoted concentration time. You have different parts inside you, and each has its own unique needs, wants, and desires. Some of these parts have been silenced for a very long time. To reawaken these voices, you will need to rebuild trust with yourself. Just like with any relationship, rebuilding trust requires authentic communication, vulnerability, empathy, openness, and the willingness to admit when you're wrong. The way you rebuild trust with yourself is to get curious, ask yourself questions, respond, listen — all out loud, of course — and give yourself what you need. The more you say it out loud to yourself, the stronger the relationship with yourself becomes.

Learn to Respect Your Reflection

I used to sit on my parents' bed watching my father get ready for work. He would massage styling cream through his hair and use a pink comb to perfectly groom himself. Watching him was so entertaining. He would look at his reflection and say out loud, "Isn't Patappa so handsome?" (Patappa is what my sister and I called our father instead of Dad.) Watching my father admire his own reflection with such confidence gave me permission to also admire and adore myself. At school, I was bullied and teased incessantly, so to have an example of self-love gave me the courage to love myself, even though so many parts of me seemed hated and unaccepted by my peers. I didn't know it at the time, but he had planted the seed for me to look at my own reflection in the mirror and talk out loud to myself. This became a daily practice for me as I entered my young adult years.

During the years that I was addicted to cocaine, I'd keep the lights off while in the bathroom because I didn't want to look at myself in the mirror. There were also rare occasions when, high as a kite, I would stand in front of the mirror with my eyes bugging out and say to myself out loud, "Vasavi, what are you doing with your life?" These experiences taught me two things:

- You can gauge your personal relationship-with-self status by standing in front of the mirror and observing your inner dialogue. As you look at your reflection, pay close attention to what the voices in your head are saying. Are you picking yourself apart? Judging every little flaw on your body and face? Tuning in to what you're saying to yourself about yourself will show you where you need to stop being self-critical and unkind.
- If you're avoiding looking into the mirror, then incorporating a combination of mirror work and Say

It Out Loud practices will help you become more authentic with yourself and others.

The more you speak your thoughts and feelings out loud, the more you can detach from them, be the observer, and transcend your critical ego's viewpoint. When you transcend the viewpoint of your ego, you can truthfully reflect on how you're feeling, the essence of your truth, and the beliefs that have been holding you hostage. Most of us spend far more time paying attention to the thoughts in our heads than we do looking at ourselves in mirrors or asking ourselves how we're feeling. Therefore, I recommend standing in front of a mirror when you practice the Say It Out Loud exercises at the end of each chapter. Look in the mirror and say what you're thinking and how you're feeling out loud. When you can look at your reflection, meet the parts of yourself that you're ashamed and embarrassed of, and verbalize out loud how these parts inside you feel, you will be able to meet others on a deeper level, because you've met yourself eye to eye.

Bring All the Parts of You to the Table

"I don't want to cause problems, so I'm just not going to say anything, but I'm so sick and tired of being treated this way, and I have to stand up for myself." Have you ever felt torn between what you want to say and what you think you "should" say? You run all your options inside your head only to exhaust yourself and just default to the thing you normally do — swallow your words or overexplain yourself.

You have different parts of you that you tap into based on the situation you're in. Think of each of these parts as subpersonalities, or different characters in your life, each with a distinct voice. These characters can come to life according to the role you are playing. For example, the voice you use when you

20

play with a baby or a puppy is very different from the voice you use in a job interview. Some voices are more encouraging than others. Some voices are louder than others. For me, my critical, harsh, and belittling voice (toward myself) was the loudest. It was the voice of my mother. I had another voice that essentially let me off the hook all the time. That was the enabling voice of my father. I have had to learn how to talk to myself using *my* voice, not the voices of my parents. I've now taken the best parts of my parents and integrated them with the best parts of myself. Those voices in your head will be externalized with the help of the exercises at the end of each chapter.

The integrative healing of all the parts within us helps us respond to life with wisdom, compassion, and confidence rather than with ridicule, judgment, and dismissiveness. Give yourself the experience of turning inward, listening to your inner voice, and cultivating a partnership with all the parts of you.

Name All the Parts of Yourself

Have you ever had a crappy day and felt like the rest of your life was doomed? (Is that even a question?) Logically you knew that wasn't true, but when one part of you is experiencing an intense emotion, the tendency might be to think that it's final and forever. It's easy to believe that one part of you makes up *all* of you. And here's what I want you to remember: You can be scared *and* courageous. You can feel guilty *and* choose you. You can feel insecure in some areas *and* be confident in other areas. All of your parts together make up your *whole being*. But if you've been in the habit of silencing some of your parts, then the way you start to build a relationship with them is to name them. For example, when I'm in an anxious state, I refer to that part of me as Vulnerable Vasavi. This part of me gets easily flustered and nervous when she feels like she is losing control of a situation.

In moments when Vulnerable Vasavi needs to be heard, I talk to her out loud and gently ask, "Vachi, I'm here for you. Talk to me. What would help you feel safe in this moment?"

On the other hand, when I'm feeling resentful and have rage brewing inside, I refer to that part of me as Vigilant Vasavi. Vigilant Vasavi has felt unheard and betrayed by people in her life. She is the part of me that exists to remind me where I have crossed my own boundaries or allowed others to step over my boundaries. Vigilant Vasavi is not about to get walked all over, and when she speaks to me, I listen to her and ask out loud, "What's making you angry right now?" When I don't give her space to be heard, she acts out. She throws tantrums. She becomes passive-aggressive. And in the past she would drown herself in drugs and alcohol. This is what happens when you exile a part of you. Sooner or later, that part will be triggered, demand your attention, and oftentimes cope in self-defeating ways.

When it comes to naming your parts, have fun and be honest. You're digging into parts of yourself that have been tucked away. As with any experience in life, choose how you want to approach learning how to talk to yourself. You get to bring the fun, playful, gentle, firm, goofy parts and whatever other characteristics you want to embody to this entire process. There is no right or wrong way to do it, simply a set of guidelines that have worked for me and many of my clients. Vulnerable and Vigilant may not be what you choose to name your parts, but this is where you start to build the relationship you have with *your* parts by naming them.

When you name your parts, you can't run from them. Pretending to be happy and stuffing your emotions are an unsustainable way of coping with life. Sooner or later, you will have to pay attention to what's going on inside you. You can't pretend to be happy when there's clearly one part of you that just needs to cry. When you say out loud, "I'm fine!" while in reality your body is screaming, "I am so not OK right now," you're misrepresenting your feelings. Physically and mentally, these inauthentic displays of emotion are costly. When you acknowledge how you really feel, say your inner thoughts out loud, and speak to yourself with kindness and respect, you're demonstrating that each part of you is worthy of your esteem and acknowledgment. And doing so will help us make healthier choices, take more risks, and courageously pursue our dreams.

Feeling, Friend, or Sage?

When you're learning how to talk to yourself, there are three ways you can address yourself: as "I," as "you," and by your first name. Your choice of which to use sets the tone for the type of conversation you're having with yourself. For example, when you say out loud, "*I* am upset right now," you're identifying with the feeling of upset. However, if you were to ask yourself, in a gentle and curious tone, "You seem upset right now. What's going on?" you'd be treating yourself more as a friend. When you use your first name — "Vasavi, talk to me. What's going on?" — you are tapping into the wise sage inside you, who can observe and guide you without getting emotionally attached.

As you go through the exercises at the end of the chapters, you will see that many of the practices and examples are in either the "I" or the "you" format. My recommendation would be to practice speaking to yourself in a way that gently moves you from feeling to friend to sage. Do not skip over expressing your feelings out loud. Start with "I" so you fully *feel* what you're experiencing. As you get more curious about what's really going on inside you, speak that thought to "you." Then, speak to yourself using your name to access guidance from your inner guru. Practice learning how to talk to yourself and have fun with the process. Play with using "I," "you," and your first name. Feel free to throw in a term of endearment, like "honeybuns"! You're in charge of how you speak to yourself. It's your voice, and you get to use it as a source of courage and comfort in your life.

Ready to say it out loud? Of course you are. Let's go.

SAY IT OUT LOUD EXERCISE

Start paying attention to your thoughts or the voices in your head. Specifically, pay close attention to how your thoughts speak to you. Do they take the form of "I," "you," or your first name? Remember, "I" is you identifying with the thought. "You" is you speaking to yourself like a friend. And when you use your first name, you're tapping into your Higher Self, the one observing what's occurring in the moment.

SAY IT OUT LOUD AFFIRMATIONS

In this moment, I am free.
There is divinity in every situation that is unfolding.
I have the intelligence and willingness to get through anything in my life.

Chapter 2

ADMIT IT OUT LOUD

Answer this out loud:
Is it hard for you to admit
that you need help sometimes?

"Hey, Vasavi! Great seeing you again!" This is how I was greeted when I went back to rehab for the second time. I was newly engaged, thirty-seven, and recently fired from my not-so-glamorous TV hosting job. I had gone from being perfectly coiffed and on-air every day for six months to being let go and, ten days later, checking myself back into rehab. I heard God say to me, "This is not the end. It's just the beginning."

I went to my counselor, Carl, and I asked him, "What do I need to do to never come back here again?" He responded, "Stop acting like you know everything, listen to what we tell you to do, and don't question anything. Just trust the process." I hated that last phrase so much. How could I trust the process when it felt like everyone around me, including me, had betrayed me?

It was clear to me I had no clue what the heck I was doing

with my life, so that was the day I admitted my powerlessness over people, places, situations, drugs, alcohol, and, most importantly, my emotions. Once I admitted my powerlessness that day, there was no more denying that my life had become unmanageable — so unmanageable, I had to check myself back into rehab. And in a way, the minute I admitted my powerlessness, I got back some of my power. I know that may sound counterintuitive, but hear me out. The minute we acknowledge and admit that we feel powerless in the face of certain people, places, and situations, we open the door to a much-needed conversation that we've been avoiding with ourselves: "I need help, and I don't know where to begin."

That day I decided to stop acting like I knew everything and started being more honest with myself. I became open to seeing my life through a different lens. As long as you're in denial, the parts of you that need your attention become your weakest link. When you acknowledge and admit that you're powerless, you open yourself up to receiving support. You're essentially saying, "I don't know what to do, and whatever I'm doing isn't working. There must be another way." Think of it like this. Have you ever tried to open a window, but your arms are too weak to even crack it a little bit? The problem isn't the window. It's that your arms are not strong enough. So you start working out and building muscle in your arms. Your arms become more powerful, and next time you try to open that window, it becomes easier. Until you decide to confront the parts of you that have been weakened by life's circumstances, you will always feel powerless. Admit your powerlessness. Get your power back.

No more hiding parts of who you are. Your power comes from acknowledging where you need to pay extra attention to the parts of you that you have pushed aside. It involves the integration of every single part of you. The intention of this chapter is to help you set the foundation for truthful dialogue with yourself by admitting out loud where you've been giving away your personal power, thus resulting in powerlessness.

> Grant me the serenity to accept the things I cannot change, the courage to change the things I can, and the wisdom to know the difference.

The Serenity Prayer is said out loud in 12-step meetings across the world, throughout the day, every single day of the week. Anyone in recovery can firmly attest to the amount of humility that it takes to admit powerlessness in the face of drugs, alcohol, sex, gambling, codependency, or whatever addiction they've given their power away to. Perhaps you've come to a point in your life where you recognize the need to stop suppressing how you feel, to start owning your truth, and to speak it out loud where it matters the most. Maybe you've been feeling ineffective and inadequate at work. Or maybe you feel like you're falling short in your relationships and friendships. But you haven't said anything because you're afraid of looking weak. Or maybe you feel the stirring of your spirit whispering to you, "You are worthy of so much more." Admitting your powerlessness requires that you put aside your pride and say out loud, essentially, "I don't have all the answers." By accepting all the things you cannot change, you open yourself up to spaciousness and the freedom to focus on what you do have control over — your thoughts, beliefs, perceptions, and actions.

The focus of this chapter is on identifying the areas of your life where you feel powerless. Extend the same level of patience and empathy to yourself that you would extend to others and allow yourself to admit out loud, "There are areas of my life where I could use some support. I don't have all the answers, and I am open to receiving guidance." It's very important that from here on out you practice being as honest as possible with yourself, out loud.

Recognizing and admitting the areas of your life in which you feel powerless requires an immense amount of humility and courage. Then, that's when the real work begins (*woo-hoo!*) — the work that most of us avoid, because, let's face it, once you admit that you feel powerless, you can't deny it any longer. From here on, the only way out of your powerlessness is to move through it like the warrior that you are. As with any journey, you need to have a clear starting point. To become the kind of person who feels confident in their skin no matter what, who can have difficult conversations, and who believes in their innate, God-given abilities to be, do, and create anything they want, you need to start by identifying the roots of your powerlessness.

Where Are You Leaking Power?

Every time we are at the mercy of external factors and relying on them to feel a sense of wholeness within, we put ourselves in the passenger seat of our life. But you don't want to ride shotgun. You want to be in the driver's seat. The way to get back into the driver's seat and stay there is to understand what I love to call your *power leakages* and how you have contributed to creating and maintaining them. Your power leakages are exactly what they sound like — areas of your life where you are leaking personal power. There are three main areas where we leak our power: self-talk, perspective, and action.

Power Leakage #1: Self-Talk

Recognize any of these statements? If so, you've been leaking power just by how you talk to yourself.

- "I can't."
- "I don't know how."
- "They won't let me."
- "No one in my family ever [went to college, started their own business, got divorced, became a millionaire, et cetera], so I can't..."
- "I'm not smart enough."
- "That's just the way it is."
- "I should just be grateful for what I have and not want more."

When you notice yourself thinking any of these limiting thoughts, pause and say that thought out loud. For example, if you hear yourself thinking, "There's no way I can get that promotion," say it out loud! And then ask yourself, "Is that actually true? Do I have evidence that there is no way I can get that promotion?" Challenge your thoughts and talk back! You may not trust that right now you can get that promotion, but you can always counteract that thought by saying, "I don't have actual evidence. This is just me doubting my capabilities once again." Respond with whatever your truth is. What you're going to discover is that what you believe you can and cannot do is simply the result of programming. You've been programmed to believe that you can't get what you want. And when you challenge all the thoughts that leave you feeling powerless, you get your power back. Don't let just a thought stop you from courageously pursuing your dreams. Taking back your power means debunking what you're telling yourself about what you're capable of.

Power Leakage #2: Perspective

The second way you might be giving away your personal power is through your perspective on life, or your beliefs. Is your perspective creating power leakages in you? Below is a list of commonly held perspectives and beliefs that might be blocking your ability to access your internal power:

- "No one cares about me."
- "What I have to say doesn't matter."
- "I have nothing to give."
- "I have no one to help or support me."
- "I'm too old to..."
- "It's too late for me to start..."

How you perceive the world around you determines how much of your personal power you're giving away. If you notice yourself taking any of these viewpoints, ask yourself out loud: "Is this true, or is this perspective based on something outside of me — my childhood upbringing, society, media, culture, religion, or social circle?" At times it may feel like everything and everyone is against you. And even in those times, you get to choose how you perceive yourself and the world around you. Powerlessness isn't a feeling. It is a choice. Choose to see every situation as an opportunity to learn more about yourself and expand your perception of what is possible, and you'll be surprised at how many doors open for you.

Power Leakage #3: Action

The third way you might be giving away your personal power is in how you take action or don't take action. How many of these statements do you identify with?

- I am resistant to change.
- I wait for circumstances to be perfect before starting anything new.
- I am waiting for someone to give me permission to do what I want.

- I procrastinate on making choices or am waiting for someone to tell me what to do.
- I don't speak up when something feels off.
- I put everyone else's needs ahead of my own.

If any of these ring true for you, it's time to get back into the driver's seat of your life — starting with admitting that one of the ways your powerlessness shows up is through the actions that you take or don't take. You start to access your power the minute you admit that you've been giving it away. Because when you admit out loud that you don't have the answers, you're acknowledging that whatever you've been doing up until this point hasn't been working. You're proclaiming out loud, "I'm ready to step into and fully own my power."

Take Personal Inventory

You will be surprised to learn that, even in the smallest of ways, you have been giving your power away. Whether it's been to the patriarchy, your family, your friends, or the thoughts in your head, take personal inventory and identify where you're giving away your power by answering the following questions. These questions are intended to help you see if how you're currently living your life is a representation of your truth or if your power is being controlled by the pressures of your thoughts, society, religion, culture, media, substances, et cetera.

Ask and answer these questions out loud:

- What are the things in my life I feel like I "should" do or feel obligated to do, even though I don't want to do them?
- What am I still holding on to?
- Where in my life am I currently being influenced by other people's opinions of me?
- Whose approval am I still seeking?

As you answer these questions out loud, notice what comes up for you. Do you feel shame or guilt? Observing your response to your responses will tell you volumes about how you treat yourself in the face of admitting your powerlessness. As I said before, it takes courage and vulnerability to admit where you don't have all the answers or where you've been giving away your power.

No one is coming to save you. Save yourself.

In Indian culture, girls go from living with their parents to becoming women and moving in with their husbands. Overnight we go from being a child to being someone's wife. Often we have very little time in between to cultivate a solid relationship with ourselves. When I got married at the age of twenty-eight, I had no idea what it meant to be my own person. I always thought that being chosen to be someone's wife was the mark of adulthood. It meant I was worth something. It meant that I was "suitable" enough for a man to want to spend his life with me. It meant I was finally settled down.

On November 28, 2010, I got married to a kind Indian man named Ashish. His name, when translated from Hindi to English, means "blessing." Our relationship was truly the biggest blessing during that period of my life. I had first met Ashish when I was in my early twenties, a sophomore in college, and in an exploratory phase in my life. He saw me for the pure soul that I was. He respected me (probably more than I respected myself) and was consistently kind. We had the big, fat Indian wedding that you've probably seen in Bollywood videos or movies like *Bend It Like Beckham*. Three days. Six hundred fifty people. A lot of mouths to feed. I thought he was my ticket to wholeness.

I will never forget what I so proudly said to the camera when our wedding videographer asked me to share a few thoughts on my new husband: "He truly saved me from myself." While it seemed romantic to me at the time, when I look back on that statement now, it's clear that I made him responsible for doing the job of loving me. I made it his responsibility to take care of me, give me attention, and push me to be better — instead of doing these things for myself.

Is there any part of you that can recognize yourself in what I'm sharing? Who are you still waiting for to save you? Think beyond marriage and partnership. At work, are you waiting for your boss to recognize that you've been putting in some serious hours, so you finally feel qualified enough to go for that next-level position in your company? Or have you been so focused on work that you haven't made any time for self-care, so you're cranky and exhausted, and you take your irritability out on your kids and partner? Where in your life have you outsourced *your* job of self-love? Admitting this out loud and taking the necessary steps to love yourself are how you get your power back.

> **Your power exists in the present moment.**

Ever have those weeks when it feels like all you're doing is putting out fires? And then the next thing you know, it's December 31 and you're thinking to yourself, "What did I even get done this year?" Now, it hits you. All your dreams on your wish list have taken a back seat in Someday Land. You know what Someday Land is, right?

- Someday I'll start…
- One of these days…
- I have other things that are more important; it can wait…
- Now's not the right time…
- I'm not ready to…
- Maybe in a few months…

When you admit out loud that you've been giving your power away to "someday," three things happen:

1. You are able to call yourself out on your own BS.
2. You start to cultivate respect for and trust in yourself.
3. You start to see that you *do* know what you need to do.

Your power exists right here, right now. Even if it's difficult for you to recognize it, I want you to know that the best time to get started on your "someday" dreams is today. Today is all you have. Your past is over. Your future has yet to be created. The most powerful (and indeed the only) time to create the most authentic version of you is now.

Own your power and be true to yourself.

We spend our entire lives trying to fit in, wearing the right clothes, driving the right car, saying things or holding back to avoid rocking the boat, all so we can feel a sense of acceptance and belonging. Be true to who you are. Drop the need to act the part. When you stop trying to keep up with a manufactured definition of success and power and instead start choosing from a place of genuine joy, you become a walking embodiment of the God within you. The love you give to yourself is greater than anything anyone can give you.

When you start to get clear on who you are and what you want out of life, you stop performing for others. You start speaking up for yourself, rather than waiting for someone to come to your rescue. You start focusing on your creative goals and cultivating new friendships with like-minded humans who support and celebrate you. Ask and answer the Say It Out Loud exercise questions out loud in front of a mirror before proceeding to chapter 3. The value of this exercise comes from being able to face yourself in the mirror, no matter how you may currently feel about yourself, and giving life to your inner voice. These questions are intended to help you admit out loud where you're giving away your power and, at the same time, guide you to take action toward regaining your internal power. Give yourself the time, attention, and space to allow your truth to emerge. Let your words move through you. It is your divine assignment to love yourself exactly the way you need to be loved in order to become the person you want to be.

These exercises are important, because they create a foundation for what we will be doing in the next chapter — examining the people, places, and situations that trigger stressful emotional responses within you. Part of learning to deal with your triggers is understanding how and why they affect you, as well as what you need in order to regulate your responses and take back your power over them.

SAY IT OUT LOUD EXERCISE

Prompt: Notice when you feel powerless, helpless, and defeated in relation to people, places, situations, and interactions. Pay attention to what you're telling yourself and how you're speaking about the situation that you're facing.

Practice: Ask and answer the following questions out loud:

- In which areas of my life am I giving away my power?
- To whom am I giving away my power?
- Am I willing to forgive myself for not knowing better?
- What's one step I can take today to step back into my power?

Promise: Promise yourself that every time you feel powerless and defeated, you won't try to minimize how you feel or sweep it under the rug. Commit to being honest with yourself about where you're giving away your power. Practice patience with yourself as you learn how to ask for help. And, most importantly, be proud of yourself. Your courage is admirable.

SAY IT OUT LOUD AFFIRMATIONS

I create space for people to support me.

I am willing to stay open to the divine guidance that moves through me, and in the form of other human beings who want to support me.

I find strength in sharing my vulnerability out loud.

Chapter 3

TALK TO YOUR TRIGGERS OUT LOUD

Answer this out loud:
What are some of the things that instantly fill you with anxiety, fear, anger, or other unpleasant feelings?

Nothing irritates me more than having to repeat myself. If there is one thing that can instantly conjure up every wound and belief I have around abandonment, this is it. Having to repeat myself brings up the beliefs that "no one pays attention to me" and "no one cares what I have to say." These beliefs were so deeply embedded in my wiring, I used to look for evidence to prove myself right. Guess what? I would find it — every time. And as long as I could find proof that my crappy beliefs about myself were in fact true, I kept my capacity for joy, pleasure, and love at a bare minimum. Nothing was going to change. The end.

Think about your own day-to-day life activities. Haven't you found that your day might start off great, but then you receive a text, or have a conversation, or a memory pops up, and you can't figure out where that great feeling went? One minute you're having a good day, and the next you're not. Your entire mood has been hijacked, and your mind keeps you hostage by replaying the distressing scenario over and over again. When left unquestioned, this one stimulus, or *trigger*, can snowball into a series of thoughts that follow you through the rest of your day.

If this has been a pattern for you, then I want you to know that you're not alone. Questioning why something triggers you and being curious about the underlying root cause will open the doors to the deeper layers of your mind and body, where you hold subconscious beliefs about who you are. We will go even deeper into your beliefs and stories in chapter 4. In this chapter, you will learn how to talk to the parts of yourself that get easily irritated. Rather than silence this part of yourself and act like everything is fine, you will learn how to be in conversation with the parts of you that haven't been given the space to express themselves, unedited.

All it takes is one trigger.

A trigger is anything external or internal that affects your mental and emotional state, thereby causing overwhelm and distress. You can be brought back to a specific event in your life through a smell, song, memory, or tone of voice that rubs you the wrong way or moves you to tears. When you're in the present moment and find yourself having an outsize reaction to what's happening externally, you're not responding to what's happening right in front of you, but to the feeling that has been stored in your body from the earliest memory or experience of that trigger.

- The person who cuts you off in traffic brings up unprocessed grief and rage from that time your boss passed you up for a long-overdue promotion.

- Someone left a jerky comment on your last Instagram post, and now you feel the same humiliation you did in the third grade, being teased in the cafeteria because you were the new girl.
- The guy you've been dating ghosts you, and you're brought back to a memory from high school when your best friend suddenly stopped talking to you without any explanation.

When you view triggers as your teachers, rather than running from people, places, and situations that get under your skin, you start to welcome and embrace those irritating moments, become curious about your internal experience, and ask out loud, "What part of me is being triggered inside, and what is it trying to tell me?" Every time you are triggered, you're being given an opportunity to get to know yourself on a deeper level. You have the chance to heal a wound that has opened up by actually checking in with yourself and interrogating what you're experiencing. You get to provide yourself with safety, security, and understanding. Here's your permission slip to get triggered. Get angry. Get sad. Feel something. Feel anything. But, for the love of all things holy, don't keep it inside.

Are You an Emotional Perfectionist?

A few years ago, I came across the term *emotional perfectionism*, and I thought to myself, "I love emotions, and I am a recovering perfectionist — tell me more!" Emotional perfectionism, coined by Dr. Annie Hickox,[*] means holding ourselves to an impossible

---

[*]   Annie Hickox, "Emotional Perfectionism: A Hidden Trigger of Anxiety," accessed December 16, 2022, http://dranniehickox.co.uk/resources -blog-neuropsychology/10-mindfulness.

standard that does not allow us to feel negative emotions, or what we perceive as negative emotions, toward anything. If you are highly uncomfortable dealing with negativity, I'm sorry to say that the solution isn't to just drown yourself in positive affirmations or sprinkle love and light all over your aura. Matter of fact, you're causing more damage to your emotional being than you may think when you bypass how you're truly feeling.

Let's look at some of the things we tell ourselves when we've just been triggered and the things we commonly say when we try to be emotionally perfect:

- "I shouldn't be mad about that."
- "Stop making a big deal. I should just get over it."
- "I can't look sad, because then people will think I'm not doing OK."
- "I can't let people know that I'm upset, because then I'll make them upset."

In other words, you have very little tolerance for your unpleasant feelings. I'm not suggesting that you sit and brood — I'm suggesting that you give yourself permission to be human, get triggered, and then use your triggers as information to get to know yourself on a deeper level. Emotionally mature, healthy individuals aren't immune to being triggered. If they get triggered by something, they allow themselves to get annoyed, check in with themselves, feel their frustration, and move through it internally or by saying it out loud. This then leads to an increase of confidence and a decrease in anxiety and depression, because they're no longer suppressing, avoiding, or denying their feelings. How you respond to yourself in those moments of irritation helps strengthen the relationship you have with yourself and your ability to respond to any situation.

Allow Your Feelings

Both the sensations in your body and the voices in your head can be overwhelming. At the very moment that you've been triggered, all logic goes out the window, leaving you feeling helpless, powerless, and dysregulated. It's like you've been taken over by a different part of you who is furiously trying to escape a dangerous situation.

Instead of trying to escape, let yourself feel however you're feeling. This is what most people avoid because they don't want to come off as being dramatic. But the truth is, whatever you get triggered by will have power over you until you can face it head-on and get to the bottom of why it bothers you so much.

Check In with Yourself

The mere act of pausing, checking in with ourselves, and talking to ourselves out loud after we get triggered slows us down and creates room for reflection and self-discovery. In those moments, we have options. We can react to our triggers and allow them to control our entire day, or we can get triggered, pause, and seek to understand what we're experiencing by asking ourselves certain questions.

Start by pausing to ask yourself, "What's bothering me?" or "What's going on inside me right now?" Allow yourself to respond truthfully with what is bothering you. Try not to filter yourself. Be as honest as you can as you share out loud what's annoying you.

Feel Your Frustration

Frustration is a normal part of the human experience, but it can be hard to put into words, especially if you're not in the habit of expressing the complicated blend of anger, frustration, disappointment, and even resentment that we experience when triggered. Commit to sitting with yourself through these mixed bags of emotions, which can feel heavy in the moment. Continue to be curious about what you're experiencing and ask yourself, "How old do I feel when I'm being triggered?" This question can help resurface memories of times when you may have experienced a similar situation, creating an entryway for you to connect with that part of yourself. Asking yourself probing questions helps you develop a deeper and more intimate relationship with yourself. Knowing the roots of what irritates you is simply giving you more information. The more you know about yourself, the more you begin to feel at home within yourself.

Move through It

You may find that you have only one trigger, but in most cases we have multiple triggers. All it takes is one comment from your coworker, one displeasing look or sigh from your mother, or one memory to send you spiraling down into the dark abyss of overwhelm, irrational thinking, and unpredictable behavior. But triggers are your friends. Your triggers show you where you need to strengthen your boundaries. They will point to the places where you can give yourself compassion and understanding. The sensations you feel because of your triggers can also help you identify your beliefs.

For example, let's say you find out that your close friend has been promoted at her job. You notice that you immediately get triggered. Your chest tightens. Maybe you think the thought "What's so great about her? How come I'm not getting promoted?" And then you spend the next few days feeling resentful toward her, annoyed with yourself, and tired from stewing in jealousy. My hope is that you won't let yourself stew in jealousy for days, but if that's the case, then this is exactly when you would practice saying out loud what it is you're experiencing.

Continuing with the example of your friend getting promoted, when you notice yourself thinking the thought "What's so great about her? How come I'm not getting promoted?" try saying it out loud and responding with whatever comes up. We're all different, but if I had to take a guess, maybe the thought that would arise for you is "You know you're not good enough. Everyone else always seems to get ahead of you." That right there is the belief that you hold about yourself.

This is where you get to channel a more curious mindset and ask, "Did you even want to get promoted? Are you happy at your job?" Or engage in a simple, gentle nudging: "OK, what's going on? Talk to me." Being curious toward yourself starts to bring more openness, inquiry, and spaciousness to the conversation you're having inside. Understanding why you get set off and irritated creates a pathway by which you can be more compassionate toward the not-so-tolerable part of you.

Let's face it, no one likes to feel irritated. It's irritating to feel irritated! But ignoring this part of you won't make it go away. It will continue to pop up in your life until you address it. And until then, you're not in the driver's seat of your life — you're at the mercy of everything that triggers you. The goal isn't to never get triggered. It's to realize that those moments when you are quick to react and lose your cool are probably great times to check in with that part of you. The trigger is not there to hurt you. You're reacting for a reason.

What Do You Believe about Yourself?

My parents were the first members of their families to immigrate to America. Almost every weekend, our house would be filled with individuals who had traveled from India and who, of course, were accommodated by my parents. I never felt like my home was my own when I was a kid. My room was normally given to whomever was staying with us at the time. I often felt like I was a nuisance and unwelcome in my own house.

One day, my mother was sitting on the couch with her two sisters, singing religious songs. Trying to get her attention, I kept tapping her knee and calling her name so I could tell her something. She didn't stop singing to acknowledge me, and eventually I gave up and walked away. That scene triggered a belief that shaped my reality for thirty-plus years: "No one cares about what I have to say." The belief that "no one cares about what I have to say" drove almost all my decisions in life. It dictated how I showed up in relationships and friendships. It determined how I walked into a room. It affected when and where I chose to say it out loud — or, more often, keep my mouth shut.

Your beliefs are the assumptions you hold to be true. They influence how you perceive yourself and the world around you. The question that I want you to start asking yourself out loud is "When and where did I first start believing [insert belief]?" to begin unraveling your current belief systems.

Beliefs Are NOT Facts

Introducing the facts and separating them from your beliefs creates room for you to question out loud, "Is this belief actually true?" Let's use the example of my belief "I do not matter." The *facts* were that my mother was singing with her sisters and I was tapping on her knee to get her attention. When she didn't respond to me, I formed the *belief* that no one cares what I have to say. Once you separate facts from beliefs, you get to tap into your wiser self and ask, "Is this belief something I still want to hold on to?" By questioning that entire scenario out loud, my wiser self was able to communicate with my inner child, the four-year-old me who thought that because her mother was lost in her own singing, I was invisible and unimportant.

Separating the facts from your beliefs does not mean that you're invalidating or minimizing how you *felt* at the time, nor does it discount any injustices that you experienced; if someone violated you, for example, that is not excusable. But how did you let your belief about the facts define you? And is that definition or belief helping you now, or is it hurting you by keeping you from who you want to become? As an adult, you have the power to question your beliefs and decide whether to keep them or change them.

You're allowed to outgrow your beliefs.

The act of questioning your beliefs will feel like you're cheating on yourself. Every part of you will want to hold on to whatever beliefs you currently have, because the beliefs you have about yourself have been with you for most of your life. Even questioning your beliefs out loud might feel uncomfortable, because you're challenging your identity. You're questioning the possibility of who you might be if you let go of these beliefs. You're essentially saying out loud, "I'm breaking up with the version of me that has been living a life according to a false set of beliefs. This doesn't work for me anymore." You're giving up your old beliefs for a set of new ones, and any part of you that still identifies with those beliefs will do whatever it takes to hold on.

But being rigid about your beliefs only keeps you disconnected from yourself and others. Questioning your beliefs out loud requires you to suspend self-judgment as you become more curious about yourself. You actually become less judgmental of yourself *and* of others when you question your own beliefs, ideas, and assumptions. Doing so will expand your capacity to be with the discomfort of challenging situations and heavy emotions. Questioning your beliefs also requires you to rise above the need to control or stay fixed in your current identity. The experiences that have shaped your beliefs up until this point no longer have to hold you back.

Confront with Care

Be patient and gentle as you talk to yourself out loud. You can also use a "keep it real" attitude when you speak to yourself, to challenge your current belief systems. For example, when separating facts from beliefs, one part of you might think, "That's not fair. What they did hurt me." That part of you will try to hold on tightly to your current beliefs and perspective, because being "right" is a way for you to protect yourself from getting hurt. Think about it. As long as you are "right" about whomever hurt you, you can keep a wall up and hold on to anger. That anger sits inside you, if not loudly then slowly brewing in the background, just waiting to be triggered so it can express itself in chaos. You can respond from the part of you that is wise beyond your years and say out loud, "I know that you must be hurt. I know it doesn't feel fair. Are you willing to be open to a new viewpoint?" And you might not be open yet. You might not be ready. But keep that dialogue with yourself going out loud, and parts of you will start to open up. Next time you can gently nudge yourself and say out loud, "Are you open to that conversation we were having the other day?" Approach questioning your beliefs out loud in the same way you would approach a friend during a respectful argument, kindly and compassionately.

It's exhausting going through life lashing out at others, always being on the defensive, and having our days, weeks, months, even years hijacked by the consequences of our reactions. By saying out loud what is triggering you, genuinely being curious, and responding, you're creating a safe space within yourself to reveal your most private thoughts. As you go through the process of talking to your triggers, you may have competing thoughts and feelings about what you're experiencing. Say those out loud too! Give yourself permission to feel everything. When responding to the question "What's triggering me right now?" don't hold back. Be as honest as possible about what's bothering you. If painful memories of conflict come to the surface, just breathe and say what you're experiencing out loud. For example, "I feel triggered because I'm comparing myself to my colleagues and how good they are at writing. It's making me think about when I was in college and my professor said that I would never become a good writer…wow, I just felt that in my chest." When you get clear on how people and situations impact you, rather than trying to defend, control, or judge the other people, you stand firmly in your power by speaking your truth. All you're doing is giving a voice to every part of you and creating space to have curious conversations with yourself… out loud.

As you go through the following exercises, remember what it was like to explore the world through the eyes of a child. The beliefs you held as a child seemed fitting at the time, but they may not fit in your current reality as an adult and where you're headed. Some of the beliefs that you explore might seem silly, but rather than trying to fix something that looks broken, focus your intention on curious self-discovery.

In the next chapter, we will look at some of the recurring themes and patterns in your life that have blocked you from emotional growth. Being able to identify and move through your triggers — as you are about to do in these exercises — is vital to this work, because many of your triggers are inextricably linked to the narratives that have run through your life.

SAY IT OUT LOUD EXERCISE

Prompt: Notice when you're feeling triggered. Pay attention to the feelings in your body. You might be feeling uneasy, resistant, and/or constrained.

Practice: Say out loud, "What's triggering me right now?" If you're not used to using the word *trigger*, other options are to say "bothering," "annoying," "irritating," or "frustrating." Once you say out loud what's bothering/triggering you, respond! Don't overthink it.

Here's an example.

"What's bothering/triggering me right now?"

"Right now, I'm triggered by the fact that my partner cut me off multiple times while I was trying to share how I was feeling about something."

"Why does my partner cutting me off multiple times trigger me?"

"It triggers me because it makes me feel like I am invisible and unworthy of their full attention."

"What do I believe about myself in those moments when my partner cuts me off multiple times?"

"I believe that I am unworthy of their full attention and presence."

Does this sound familiar? How quickly do you focus on the other person when you're triggered? As you begin to ask yourself questions, you'll start to see that nearly everything you get triggered by has nothing to do with the other person. In the dialogue above, the focus was initially on her partner. But as she began to go deeper, she realized that her partner's way of interacting with her exacerbated a belief she had held about herself for a very long time. Her newfound awareness of her beliefs didn't excuse her partner from cutting her off while speaking. But it enabled her to get her personal power back so that she could focus on rewriting her beliefs and story (more on this in the next chapter), get clear on her boundaries and desires for communication, and be able to say all of that out loud to her partner.

Promise: Promise yourself that anytime you feel triggered, you will pause and check in with yourself, rather than react in a way that leaves you feeling depleted. Commit to seeing your triggers as the gateway to understanding yourself on a deeper level.

SAY IT OUT LOUD AFFIRMATIONS

I'm going to be patient with myself no matter what I am experiencing in this moment.

My triggers are my teachers. They show me where I need to deepen my understanding of myself.

I observe my negative thoughts, and I easily clear them out.

Some days will be harder than others. That's OK. I will get through them.

Chapter 4

TRANSFORM YOUR STORY OUT LOUD

Answer this out loud:
What are some situations that you find yourself stuck in over and over again?

When I was nineteen years old, I was given a diagnosis of bipolar disorder. I was told that I would be on medication for the rest of my life. I went from telling myself, "I'm too much" to "I'm clinically crazy" overnight. It was a huge relief. I had spent the first two years of college partying, sleeping around, and doing way too many drugs. I knew that what I was doing was out of character for me. (But was it really? Or was this a part of myself that needed to be expressed?) What I had thought was maybe just me being highly energetic and emotional now had a label slapped onto it. It was a relief because I suddenly felt like there was absolutely nothing wrong with me. With the diagnosis, my young adult actions no longer felt shameful; instead, I was relieved that who I was could finally fit into a box — a box created by Western medicine and labeled as "bipolar disorder."

Being naturally curious, I headed to the nearest bookstore and devoured all the books I could find related to bipolar disorder. One stood out to me: *The Tao of Bipolar* by C. Alexander Simpkins. What I came to understand was that the "bipolarity" within me was nothing more than the never-ending conflict between my Higher Self and my ego. I was neither manic nor depressed. I was in a constant state of struggle between who I knew I was at the core and who I thought I "should" be.

I found healing from bipolar disorder by choosing to re-write the narrative of what "happened" to me. I could have let my bipolar diagnosis be the story that ran my life. And for much of my life, I did. I would tell myself that I was defective because I was given a bipolar disorder diagnosis. If I ever felt really excited about something, I would tell myself to calm down because I didn't want to come off as too manic or bipolar. Or if I felt deeply moved to tears by something, I would tell myself to keep it together so I didn't appear highly emotional or unstable. As I came to understand my mind and my thoughts, connect with my body, and say my thoughts out loud, I was able to transform how I viewed my diagnosis. I chose to see my bipolar disorder, not as something that "happened" to me, but as an opportunity to know myself on a deeper level. Being given a diagnosis that clearly stated I was split within was the biggest gift I could have ever received. It challenged me and fueled me to experiment with many different paths to come back *home* to myself. To become *one* with myself.

When we are born, we come into this world whole and complete. We do not come with baggage; we typically accumulate that as adults. When you entered this world, you were curious, inquisitive, and eager to soak in all that life had to offer. And then ... something happened. A part of you energetically split off from your body, though it never fully left you. The part of you that split off was innocent, curious, playful, and open. This is what I refer to as your *inner child* through the book. The things that "happened" are what I refer to as your *triggers* (see chapter 3), and they skewed your perception of reality. You began to see the world through the lens of fear, rejection, punishment, abandonment, and betrayal. What "happened" made you acutely aware of who and what types of energy you felt safe/unsafe with. It informed you of exactly what to do/not to do and who to be/not to be, so you would never have to feel pain again. The most toxic voice in our lives, the one that holds us back more than the opinions of others, is our own critical narrative. You need to learn how to reduce the volume of that voice within, the one that is discouraging, fear based, and hypercritical of you, because it is often the loudest one in your mind.

As you continued to move through life, adapting, accommodating, and avoiding anything that would make you feel pain again, you believed you had to protect yourself in order to feel safe. You protected yourself by hiding parts of you, staying under the radar, and never being "too much" or too loud. At work, you didn't pitch your ideas, even though you had a ton of them, because you didn't think they were good enough. Or you held back from building key partnerships and other relationships because you believed that people wouldn't like you or would think you were not good enough. See all these beliefs? All your beliefs become the *stories of your life*. These stories are the patterns you continue to experience over and over again. They form the narrative by which you live, interact, communicate, create, and connect with others and yourself.

Your stories are the "this is what happened" regarding all of the experiences that you've had throughout your entire life.

Your stories shape everything in your life, from what you wear to how you show up in social settings to how close you allow yourself to get to others. Your stories are there to protect you from the things that "happened," to keep those things from ever happening again. You are the creator of your life stories. That is why, in this chapter, you will learn how to identify the patterns that have run your life up until this point. By identifying the narrative that has been running your life, you can start to question whether that narrative is in alignment with who you want to become and start to transform it out loud. The goal of this chapter is to show you that your words have the power to create new life stories, stories that are expansive, supportive, and able to guide you toward the person you were born to be.

> **The more you believe your stories,**
> **the more they become your reality.**

From the time we are born, we are told who we are, who we are not, what we should do, and how we should do it. And not to question any of it! We nod our heads up and down like bobbleheads, soaking up every message that is thrown our way. As a result, we go through life believing everything our minds tell us and never question the adage "That's just the way things are." Some of us aren't even aware that we've been programmed to just believe everything that is being fed to us. Or when we do have the courage to question what we're told, we're labeled as being "too much" or "aggressive" for just being naturally curious. That's the thing about our beliefs. They're deeply embedded in our minds. When the voices in our heads remain verbally unexpressed, they become the fixed truth of our reality.

We all make up stories in our heads based on circumstances and cues, both verbal and nonverbal, and then begin to believe the stories our minds have made up. Your boss responds to your email with a one-liner and no smiley face, and you wonder, "Are they mad at me? Am I in trouble?" In reality, your boss was probably overburdened with work, wanted to acknowledge your email, and was quick to move on to their next task. Or your partner comes home from work, and instead of going into the kitchen to kiss you on the cheek, they go straight upstairs, and you think to yourself, "I don't even matter to them." But maybe, just maybe, your partner had a long day and needs five minutes alone to recharge before returning downstairs to spend time with you.

The unspoken narrative in your mind carries as much weight as the narrative you say out loud. That's why every exercise in this book guides you to say your innermost thoughts out loud. When you repeatedly think the same beliefs and run the same stories, you accept them as the truth. When you say these same narratives out loud, you will begin to differentiate between what happened and what you're telling yourself happened. When you keep your stories in your head, you're quite literally *in* your stories. But when you say them out loud, they're *out of you*; this creates distance between you as the main character of your story and you as the creator of your life. Being able to discern between the facts and the stories will create space for you to take a more integrated approach to your life, using both logic and emotion.

Notice Your Stories

Every single one of your stories is intended to keep you safe from rejection and humiliation. But what often happens is that these same stories perpetuate the cycle of shame and self-condemnation. There is a part of us, the deep knowing that exists inside each and every one of us, that is acutely aware of how we're getting in our own way. No matter how much we try to numb ourselves and disconnect from our deep knowing, it never leaves us. I know this because even in the depth and darkness of my addiction, I always heard a voice that said to me, "Stop hurting yourself." This was my voice of reason and genuine concern. We cannot outrun the voices in our head, even the quietest ones. We free ourselves from our shame by saying out loud, "I'm no longer allowing this story to control my life. I'm ready to create a new story."

Pay attention to what you're telling yourself about what you're experiencing throughout the day. When a thought comes up about something or someone, notice the story you have. Also pay attention to how you speak about the different scenarios in your life. Notice how you speak about *other* people and their lives and how they "should" or "shouldn't" be.

Read the following statements out loud and count how many you identify with:

- "I can't be vulnerable — I'll just get hurt."
- "I'm better off on my own."
- "I'm not worthy."
- "I'm too much for anyone to handle."
- "I don't deserve to be happy."
- "I'm weak/inadequate."
- "I'm so bad at…"
- "I can't ever be too happy, because then it will go away."
- "I'm a failure."
- "I should be farther along."
- "Asking for help makes me look weak/stupid."

How many of these narratives did you identify with? Every narrative you identify will help you gain access into deeply held beliefs that have been stunting your fullest self-expression. Let's use the eighth one as an example: "I can't ever be too happy, because then it will go away." If you've been telling yourself this, a few things are predictable. You won't ever allow yourself to be happy, because you've already told yourself you can't be. You will allow people into your life who always manage to leave you feeling worse about yourself. And you will seek out situations that perpetuate the narrative you have about yourself.

Our stories are the lens through which we look at life. So if you've attached a filter to your lens that is the story "People always abandon me," your subconscious mind will seek to be abandoned. On a logical level, this makes no sense, right? Why would you intentionally seek out a story that ends up with you as the abandoned one? Who would deliberately try to create a reality where they ended up being the victim (or the villain)? Here's why. Our emotions get stored in our body. And until we give our unexpressed emotions a voice and release them out of our body through our words, they will continue to stimulate re-actions from us, all while continuing to perpetuate our stories.

Our stories can come from anywhere and anyone. If you've had bosses who have undermined you, then the next time you apply for a job, you might go in with the narrative "This job is probably going to be just as bad as the last one, because all bosses are jerks." In the end, rather than shoot for a job that is exciting and new for you, you stay in the same job because your narrative has you believing that no matter what, your job is going to suck because "all bosses are jerks." If you had a parent who made sure to let you know when you gained a few pounds, you might be an adult who is critical of your body and have a story that sounds like, "I'm unlovable because I've gained weight." Or if you had a parent who made blanket statements like, "All women are bossy and controlling" or "All men are dogs," you may start to view certain types of women as bossy and controlling, when in reality the women you're surrounded by are simply assertive and direct in their communication, or you might believe that no man can be trusted.

No matter how painful your stories are and how much they limit you, you hold on to them because they feel *familiar*. For example, we keep going back to certain types of people even though we know that they aren't healthy for us. Or we take a job we know we're not going to enjoy, because we've told ourselves, "There are no good jobs out there." Or maybe we have an entrepreneurial spirit and want to start a business, but we keep hearing this story in our heads that informs us, "You aren't smart enough." Anytime you attempt to break away from your narrative and do something that is unfamiliar, your old, familiar story will creep in. Your story isn't "bad" or "good." Your story, as I mentioned earlier, is there to protect you from ever again having to face what "happened." But at some point we have to stop and ask ourselves out loud, "Am I willing to break this recurring pattern in order to have the life that I have always wanted?"

> Everything we do in our life has a payoff, including telling ourselves stories about who we are.

Don't Get Stuck in Your Stories

Sara grew up with a father who struggled with addiction and a mother who enabled him. Sara took on the role of emotional caregiver for her family early in her life. Her high-functioning and overachieving ways led her to land her dream job, buy her dream house, and receive numerous professional accolades. She hoped that by doing all these things, her family of origin, husband, and colleagues would recognize, applaud, and acknowledge her. She was sadly mistaken. The lack of acknowledgment from her family and friends only fueled her to do more.

We worked together for several months to unravel her narrative, which was: "I need to do more in order to receive love, money, and happiness." Her narrative presented itself in most of the areas of her life. In her career, she had climbed her way to the top, but she was burned out. In her marriage, she was carrying the emotional burden for both her and her husband instead of voicing her needs clearly. In the business she had recently started, she craved more creative self-expression but felt paralyzed by the fear of other people judging her.

One day she said, "I don't understand. I know my story is keeping me stuck. Why is it so hard for me to let go of it?" Here's how I responded, and it is the question I want you to ask yourself out loud: "What payoff do I get from the stories I tell myself?"

If you can't come up with an answer right away, that is OK. Our stories are so deeply embedded that we come to think of them as the core of who we are. We identify with our stories, so asking ourselves what the payoff is seems counterintuitive. After all, these stories have been the script, the recurring pattern, of your life, and you've tolerated them (up until now). Why on earth would you continue to tell yourself a story that is unhelpful and holds you back from your dreams, goals, and desires?

Let's look at the payoff of Sara's narrative, "I need to do more in order to receive love, money, and happiness." When I asked her what the payoff was, she immediately responded, "Payoff? What payoff would I get out of telling this story to myself? I'm tired and burned out and sick of everything. What payoff could there possibly be?"

What I asked her next is what I want you to ask yourself out loud: "Is this story getting me closer to the truth of who I am?"

Every story you have told yourself (and believed) has influenced the person that you are today. The payoff is that if you allow this story of yours to go unquestioned, you won't have to be completely honest with yourself and take 100 percent responsibility for your life. Your stories are seductive; they let you off the hook. Your time, energy, and attention will always be focused on the other characters in your story and the drama that goes along with it. And let's be real, change is hard. Letting go of the person we used to be isn't for the faint of heart. In order for you to step into the fullest expression of yourself, you're going to have to let go of thoughts, beliefs, and patterns that have grown familiar. As long as your story is alive, a part of you will remain split from yourself. To reconnect the part of yourself that split, you need to transform the story that caused the split in the first place. You will continue to feel disconnected from yourself until you confront your stories and commit to rigorous honesty. But when you breathe life into a more empowered story, it has the capacity to bring you closer to the truth of who you are.

Soften Your Approach with Yourself

The second time I was in rehab, I worked closely with a counselor who was kind and didn't hold back on giving me straight feedback. I appreciated her honest and direct approach during one particular session, when I spent the first twenty minutes ranting about my ex-boyfriend.

"My ex really messed me up. I wouldn't be here again if he didn't treat me like a doormat. Do you know how many times he's cheated on me? How much money I've spent on him? How much time and energy I've wasted on him? And for what? Look at what he did to me. I'm pathetic."

I could tell she was thinking carefully about what she would say next. "If you knew he was cheating and felt that you were wasting your time, energy, and money on him, why did you allow it to continue? Instead of focusing on him and what he did, how about starting with why you continued to allow this type of behavior and treatment in your life?"

I began to soften. It wasn't just the content of the question that she asked me, it was *how* she asked me. I didn't feel judged, attacked, or small in that moment. Her approach was so gentle and curious, my nervous system relaxed. Suddenly, this story that had become a hard, protective shell around me began to melt. I didn't feel the need to keep holding on to it. Her kind approach helped shift my focus from the ex-boyfriend, whom I had made out to be the villain of my story, onto me. I become more curious.

That one question asked out loud helped transform my story that day. I kept asking myself, "Vasavi, why did you continue to allow this type of behavior?" throughout the day. I was no longer focused out there, on my ex-boyfriend; I had turned inward. And by turning inward and continuing to talk to myself out loud, I realized that I allowed this type of behavior because that is all I thought I was worth receiving.

My "unworthy story" didn't stop with love. I reconsidered how I thought about the amount of money I believed I was worthy of and how much happiness and connection I allowed myself. My narrative was "I am not worthy of more." So when I set out to transform my narrative out loud, I practiced asking myself, "What's your new story around your worth?" and I responded with, "I am worthy of and open to receiving *all* of the love." I said that every day out loud, until I started to *feel* it. When I felt that I was worthy *from the inside*, I knew my story had transformed, because no part of me questioned my worth and value anymore. And on the days when I do question my value, I know just how to tap back into the part of me that undoubtedly knows my worth.

One question can change the trajectory of your life. When you take the time to communicate with yourself out loud and commit to noticing your stories, calling them out, and becoming gentle and curious toward them, then there is no way you will not transform your life. Changing the ways you speak to yourself, coupled with curiosity and a loving approach, can soften even the most hardened of hearts and the most deeply embedded of inner narratives.

Take Inventory of Your Stories

Look at the different areas of your life one by one — your social life, relationships, career, finances, creativity, overall fulfillment — and ask yourself out loud: "What's the story I'm telling myself about [insert area of life]?"

Let's use finances as an example. Say you're not happy with how much money you're bringing in every month. Just as you give wise and kind advice to your friends, clients, and colleagues, you can tap into that part of yourself and shift into a softer energy when talking to yourself out loud. Remember, it's not just what you say, it's how you say it, out loud.

When you ask yourself out loud, "What's the story I'm telling myself about making money?" pause and listen for the next thought that comes up. Say that out loud. It might sound something like, "I'm telling myself that I'm not smart enough to make the kind of money I want to make." From there you can begin to ask more curious questions to unpack your narrative. In response to "I'm telling myself that I'm not smart enough to make the kind of money I want to make," try asking yourself, "Do you really believe you're not smart enough?" Practice being as honest as you can with the intention of uncovering and freeing yourself from your stories. This question will then prompt your next thought, which you will say out loud: "Yes. I don't actually think I'm good at anything. I have a lot of good qualities, and I'm a good person, but I don't really know what I'm smart at." Once again, you get to respond: "Are you open to digging deeper into this story?" At this point you're looking to gauge your willingness to transform your story and say, "Yes!" out loud!

Challenge Yourself to Transform

The questions you ask yourself are intended to challenge you to look at yourself objectively, which is much harder to do when you keep your stories in your head and they become your identity. When you say it out loud, you can hear the fallacies that you've been telling yourself and believing. Once you hear those fallacies, you get to push back against your story to test its accuracy. Returning to the last example, you would ask yourself out loud, "Do you have any proof that you are not smart?" or "What is your definition of *smart*?"

Challenge your stories out loud, with interest. All those questions you had but didn't feel comfortable asking throughout your life? You're now able ask them. What you will learn is that the stories you've been telling yourself don't belong to you. They belong to every single person with whom you've crossed paths, all of whom have had some impact on how you viewed yourself, your abilities, your potential, and your worth. You now get to rewrite your narrative by challenging your old stories. You're becoming conscious of the fact that all the things you've been telling yourself (and that have been holding you back) simply aren't true. Now you have the spaciousness to rewrite your story into one that will guide you to who you want to become.

Your new story can be whatever you want it to be.

The stories that you uncover will start to lose the control they once had over you. Now you get to take back your life and say out loud, "I am ready to transform my story, because the one I currently have is no longer aligned with where I am headed." Let's go back once more to the story of not being smart enough. You can transform that into your new story simply by saying out loud, "I am excellent at understanding people. Among my best traits and skills are my empathy and my ability to be an active listener." Write your new and much improved story on colorful sticky notes and tape them on your mirrors throughout your house. As you walk by them during the day, speak the new story out loud while looking into the mirror, or say it out loud like a mantra when you're taking a walk in the morning.

It's Simple, Not Easy

Is the process of changing our narrative as simple as revisiting our past and questioning everything we've heard and been told? Yes and no. Yes, because when we drop our resistance to changing our narrative, we open the doors to creating a life beyond our wildest imagination. No, because our mind wants us to stick with the current narrative. Your current narrative keeps you stuck right where you are, constantly living on the brink of stepping into a new chapter of your life. It keeps you safely protected from being hurt again. It also keeps you from outgrowing others and walking away from relationships that no longer serve you. Any attempt to try something new will be met with roadblock after roadblock — the biggest one being your narrative about what's possible.

Every day you have the power to choose the stories that you tell yourself. Interrupting the pattern of your narrative is as simple as asking yourself out loud, "Is this narrative helping me or hurting me?" and "Am I willing to see this differently?" Prompting yourself to answer these questions out loud begins the dialogue about whether the narrative you have is in alignment with the person you are becoming. We need to tell ourselves a new story, one that will lead to us closing the split within ourselves.

It is your birthright to write a new story.

Anything and everything you are going through or have gone through can be healed when you learn to become one with who you are. The truth of who you are resides in the deep knowing that no matter what you have gone through, a part of you has always stayed with you through all the ups and downs. Your voice will help you regain access to the truth of who you are. And when you hear what you've been saying to yourself, you'll be able to shift into your empathy and use your free will to reconnect to your truth. Remember, the longer you keep the voice in your head unexpressed, the truer it will feel for you. The minute you say how you feel out loud, you can detach from the stories that have held you back and become the loving mother, father, therapist, healer, coach, and best friend to talk to through any situation.

You have many different parts inside that you can tap into as you begin to transform your story out loud. Who you become through the process of saying it out loud *is* the transformation. Stay focused on speaking kindly to yourself. All it takes is one simple question asked with gentleness and curiosity to bring your nervous system to a calm state. From there you can access the compassionate, wise, sage-like energy that you possess to help you transform your narrative, out loud. When you are deeply connected to the truth of who you are, nothing and no one can ever abandon you, because you always have you.

In chapter 5, we will focus on expressing your emotions out loud, building directly on the work we have just done. Your emotions are in many ways a product of the story line that you have created about your life and the themes that define it. Thus, a deep understanding of the feelings you have toward your ever-changing life story is important.

SAY IT OUT LOUD EXERCISE

Prompt: Notice the stories you tell about yourself to yourself, as well as the stories you tell about the people, places, and things you come across. Pay attention to what you're telling yourself about what you're experiencing throughout the day. When a thought comes up about something or someone, simply notice your inner narrative, or the story you have about it.

Practice: Identify your story out loud and from there, notice what you're saying to add fuel to your fire. Ask and answer out loud, "What's the story that I am telling myself about this situation?"

Here's an example: Let's say an external trigger sets off your critical internal narrative.

"What's the story that I am telling myself about myself?"

"I wasted so much of my life, and now I'm too old to even make a difference. What is the point?"

"What payoff do I get from telling myself that story?"

"Well, as long as I tell myself that I've wasted so much of my life and I'm too old to make a difference, I won't go after my dreams."

"Does this story support the life I am creating?"

"No. It just keeps me scared and right where I am. I know that I have so much inside me to give, yet my stories tell me that it's too late."

"Am I willing to look at my situation from a kinder and more open-minded perspective?

"Yes."

"OK, great! What would I say to a friend who said, 'I wasted so much of my life, and now I'm too old to even make a difference. What is the point?'"

(This is where you get to tap into the wise, empathetic, and compassionate part of you.)

"I would say to them that everything you go through in life shapes you to become who you are. You have so many lessons you have learned throughout your life, and it is never too late to make a change in your life. As long as you are alive, anything is possible!"

"OK, great. Say that out loud to yourself."

Now say exactly what you would say to a friend out loud to yourself and insert your first name instead of "I."

"[Insert your first name], everything you go through in life shapes you to become who you are. You have so many lessons you have learned throughout your life, and it is never too late to make a change in your life. As long as you are alive, anything is possible!"

You have the power to transform your narrative when you're open to changing it — when *you* decide you've had enough of the current narrative in your life. Commit to seeing yourself differently. Open your heart to yourself.

Promise: Promise to be gentle as you get curious about the stories you tell yourself about yourself and other people. Commit to being open about whether your stories are helping you get closer to your truth or farther away from it. Give yourself permission to outgrow old narratives that you've been holding on to. Gently remind yourself that it is safe for you to grow.

SAY IT OUT LOUD AFFIRMATIONS

I am the creator of my life story.
I free myself from any unhelpful ideas, thoughts, and stories about myself.
I accept radical responsibility for creating a life that deeply satisfies me.

Chapter 5

EXPRESS YOUR EMOTIONS OUT LOUD

Answer this out loud:
If you gave your emotions a voice,
what would they say?

I had the awareness at the age of twelve that if I didn't express my emotions out loud, I would eventually implode. My mother found a cigarette in the toilet, which I swiftly covered for by saying that I had been cleaning up the backyard and found cigarette butts. She didn't buy my story for a second. Neither of my parents drank or smoked, so for them to find out that their twelve-year-old daughter was smoking was absolutely devastating. My mother said, "You're going to be the reason why your father dies of a heart attack." Clearly, she didn't know how to process her own emotions and just said how she felt, without realizing the impact her words would have on me.

Later that evening, my parents and I were in the kitchen, and I emphatically said out loud, "I can't talk to either one of you! I need someone who will listen to what I'm saying!" I knew that if I didn't get some sort of support in my life, I would lose my mind. My father's younger brother had recently killed himself, so the thought of his own daughter going down a similar path was enough motivation for my father to ask a client of his to recommend a therapist for me.

Enter Virginia.

In my very first therapy session, Virginia asked me to draw a picture of my family. I drew my father with a briefcase, my older sister reading a book, me as a tiny stick figure, and my mother as a big, overshadowing person towering over the three of us, screaming. Virginia asked me, "How do you feel inside you when you look at this picture?" With tears welling up in my eyes, I said, "I don't feel like I belong in my family. I am scared of my mother, and my father doesn't do anything to stop her." It was the first time I had been asked to connect with my internal experience and encouraged to express it out loud.

In therapy, I felt safe enough to share my deepest feelings with Virginia. I could say exactly how I felt, without judgment. She used a calm, soothing tone of voice with me. Her voice helped me even between sessions, because as I experienced emotions in my body, I learned how to talk to myself the way Virginia would talk to me: by asking myself questions with kindness and from a place of genuine curiosity. She helped me learn how to understand my emotional needs and how to express my boundaries, even with my parents. The one key question that she asked during every one of our sessions was, "Vasavi, what do you need to feel safe?" And every time I would respond with, "I just need someone to listen to me without making me feel crazy for feeling the way that I do."

Every week for sixteen years, I practiced expressing my feelings, learning how they felt in my body, and making sense out of my bundle of emotions. In doing so, I gained perspective on people and situations that had a hold over my peace and sanity. I trusted Virginia, who guided me to see things differently. If you struggle with expressing your emotions out loud, it's not because you don't have any, or you're numb, or you're an empty shell of a human being. Far from it. You just haven't learned what you need to feel safe inside your body in order to express your emotions out loud. Knowing and expressing your boundaries is what will help you restore safety within your body. When you practice saying it out loud to yourself, you can communicate your emotions and boundaries with others. As we give ourselves the space to rest our minds, feel into our bodies, and say out loud what we're experiencing, we begin to unburden ourselves from intergenerational trauma that has been passed down to us from a young age.

My friend Richelle once said to me, "It's in the quietest of moments that our bodies begin to heal." By slowing down, connecting with your body, and giving a voice to your feelings out loud, you'll begin to be the safe space for yourself. In chapter 3, you started noticing and acknowledging your triggers. You started becoming aware of the things that irritate you and saying them out loud. You were able to identify which of your beliefs were at the core of your triggers. In this chapter, you will learn the four ways that your mind hijacks your feelings, as well as how to express your emotions out loud so that you can create boundaries to feel safe within.

Stop Intellectualizing Your Feelings

When your tooth hurts, you go to the dentist. When your car needs to be fixed, you go to the mechanic. When you want to save money, you put yourself on a budget. These are all problems that can easily be fixed. It doesn't work that way with your emotions. You can't fix your feelings by numbing, minimizing, or dismissing your experience. In fact, you'll probably end up feeling worse.

A common coping mechanism that we develop to avoid painful feelings is intellectualizing them. By turning our feelings into ideas and concepts, we never have to fully feel them. If you tend to answer the question "How do you feel?" with "I *think* I feel…" then it's fair to say that you tend to intellectualize your feelings. How do I know this? Because this used to be me. I spent a great deal of time in therapy, processing my emotions and try-ing to make sense out of how I felt. I often left feeling exhausted because it took so much mental energy for me to understand the bigness of my emotions. To cope with that bigness and not be "too much" for those around me, I learned how to package my emotions so that they were more digestible to others. The more I did this, the less connected I felt to all the parts of me.

This isn't to say that your mind is not useful. Please, feel your feelings, but also use your logic. The problem comes when you rely too heavily on your mind to understand your feelings. When you do that, you're leaving behind parts of you that reside in your body. Reconnecting with your body, noticing when you feel something, and talking to your body are as simple as asking yourself out loud, "What am I experiencing in this moment?" and then answering that out loud. Don't worry about how you sound or if the words that you are using are "good" or "smart" or "make sense." That is just your mind wanting you to look and sound a certain way, in order to be accepted by others. Seek to understand yourself first and foremost.

Let Your Body Speak to You

When you need to go to the bathroom, do you hold it in, or do you get up and go the minute your body signals to you? Or maybe you ignore the sensation and tell yourself you can hold it in...until you no longer can, and you end up scrambling to find the nearest restroom. Now, listen, your digestion is your business. And while this example might have made you cringe or giggle, I want you to think of your body, and particularly your voice, as the channel through which you express your emotions. It is important to express your emotions out loud because you are a creative conduit. The things that you're keeping inside you clog you up. If your conduit is clogged, your creativity cannot move through you freely.

To receive guidance from your inner self and allow your ideas to flow unencumbered, you need to express your emotions out loud. Because every time you bottle your emotions up instead of saying them out loud, your channel gets clogged. Unexpressed emotions suck up your energy and leave you with nothing to offer to yourself, your creativity, or your loved ones. You're here on this planet to be the highest and truest expression of yourself, and you can't be that when your creative channel is backed up.

Thinking exhausts you. Feeling expands you.

The key to connecting with your body is to stop *thinking* about your feelings and start *feeling* and *expressing* them out loud. You can easily spot when you're intellectualizing your feelings (rather than feeling them), especially when you tell, argue, package, or rationalize with your mind about how you feel.

Telling Yourself: "Don't feel this way."

You find out that your friend got promoted. You immediately feel jealous, but then you tell your mind, "Don't be jealous of my friend." Has telling yourself *not* to feel a certain way ever worked? Does that feeling ever go away? No, it doesn't. Most likely, anytime you see that friend, you feel a distance between you and them because you haven't sat with your jealousy and allowed yourself to feel it. The energy of jealousy gets activated when you are around this friend because you haven't processed it out loud with yourself.

Notice when you tell yourself not to feel a feeling. Ask out loud, "Where in my body do I feel jealousy?" Observe where you feel it. Pause, breathe in and out, and place your hand on your body where you feel jealousy. If you feel jealousy in your chest, then express that out loud: "I feel my jealousy in my chest." Place your hand on your chest to connect with that part of you. And then ask yourself, with curiosity, "If my jealousy had a voice, what would it say in this moment?" Pause, breathe in and out, and allow the words to surface. Don't push yourself to come up with the "right" words. Just be patient and wait. They will come. Maybe they say, "I feel like I should be farther along." This is where you get to be a friend to yourself and probe gently: "Can you share more with me?" Rather than telling yourself not to feel, get yourself to open up to you.

Arguing with Yourself: "I shouldn't feel this way."

Any time a relationship of mine ended, I would spend a solid year and a half dragging it out afterward, mentally arguing, role-playing, and reliving every single conversation, permutation, and combination of outcomes my former partner and I might have gone through. I thought that I could have been better or more understanding. Or I would argue with thoughts of my partner, out loud: "Well, maybe you should have paid more attention when I was talking?!" I would become so invested in arguing with my thoughts that the only way to snap myself out of it was to say out loud, "Vasavi, get out of your head and into your body." I thought that by obsessing and arguing with my mind about how things "should" have been or "could" have been, I was healing. The truth was, arguing with my mind protected me from having to feel the pain of the breakup.

Notice when you're arguing with the thoughts in your mind. Start becoming aware of when you disconnect from your physical body. Gently ask yourself, "Are you in your head or your body?" Be honest with yourself. To get back into your body, take a deep breath and then exhale with a sound: "Ahhhhh." Allow yourself to soften. Breathe again. You will feel yourself melting back into your body. When you're feeling more grounded, ask yourself, "How do you feel?" Allow your feelings to speak through you, expressing them out loud: "I feel..."

If you do not have the words (yet) to give a name to your feelings, you can also describe them using colors, images, sounds, textures. When I was younger, I wasn't equipped with the vocabulary to name my feelings, but I was able to create visuals for myself. For example, when I held a lot of anger internally, I would often describe it as a solid black rock with very tiny pores. The point is everyone's feelings speak to them differently. Your body and you have a sacred relationship. Be patient as you're learning to understand the language of your emotions.

Packaging Your Feelings: "It's OK, I'm fine."

The best advice I have ever received came from my acting coach, who said to me, "Stop talking over your emotions like they're not there." I would often gloss over my emotions because I couldn't sit with the discomfort of feeling that maybe I was a burden to others. If you tend to package your feelings, you might say something like, "I had a really bad day, but it's OK. I'll be fine. What are we eating tonight?" or "I'm hurt, but whatever, it is what it is." We unconsciously package how we feel to make our emotions comfortable for others, but mostly because we are not comfortable fully feeling our feelings.

What I want you to know is that you will find emotional freedom with others and in yourself when you stop packaging how you express your feelings. Notice when you find yourself packaging how you feel. Look out for statements such as:

- "It's not a big deal."
- "I don't want to burden you."
- "I'll stop rambling."
- "Ugh, I'm so sorry. I feel like such a mess."

When you notice any statements that water down the expression or intensity of your emotions, ask yourself out loud: "What would the truest expression of my feelings sound like if I stopped packaging them for myself or others?" Asking this out loud will interrupt your pattern. Anytime you observe yourself getting sucked in by your thoughts, use that as an opportunity to guide yourself back into your body. Remember, you cannot think your way into feeling your feelings.

Rationalizing Your Feelings: "I'm not upset that I didn't get the promotion. It would be too much work anyway."

We have all encountered someone in our life whom we should have walked away from years ago but we couldn't muster up the courage. Most likely, it was because we rationalized how we felt about them. Whether it was that cynical friend from college, or that colleague who loved to take all the credit for our work, or our partner who developed a habit of emotionally dumping all over us, we rationalized the impact of their actions on our emotional well-being. If your inclination is to rationalize your feelings, then you might say things like, "It's fine — they were having a bad day" or "It's my fault. I shouldn't make such a big deal out of it." The long-term effects on your mental, emotional, and physical health go beyond anxiety and worry. All these rationalized feelings need to land somewhere, and left unexpressed, they get stored in your body as stuck energy.

Notice when you're rationalizing your emotions. Pay attention to how unresolved you feel even after rationalizing. You'll feel like you haven't fully processed your emotions, because you cannot lie to your body, and your body will always find a way to communicate your feelings to you. In those moments, ask yourself out loud, "Is there anything left unsaid about how I feel?" Respond out loud. Probe with care and with the intention of becoming more honest and connected with how you feel, rather than using rationalization to cope. The intention is to move you from your rational mind down into your emotional body. This is a moment-to-moment practice to begin integrating every part of you, so that you're not just operating from the neck up.

Expand Your Self-Soothing Toolbox

"I'm afraid of something bad happening. That's why I've got to stay on my toes. I'm scared that if I slow down, I won't be prepared if something bad happens." This is what my client said to me over a voice note. She had just completed a huge week for her business and personal brand. She was receiving more exposure than before, and people were starting to recognize her. She garnered three speaking invitations over the course of two weeks, which meant even more visibility for her business.

When she showed up for our weekly call, I could feel her exhaustion and suggested she take a few days to rejuvenate. The thought of slowing down was out of the question for her. She had created so much momentum in her life, she was caught up in the doing of things, and stopping was unthinkable. When she slowed down enough to catch her breath on our weekly call, that was what she needed to say out loud. Her need for speed started in adolescence, when she was told her parents were getting divorced. She witnessed her mother throwing herself into work to avoid dealing with her own heartbreak. So, as an adult, that's what my client did too. She threw herself into her work. And while her work gave her a sense of purpose, it never quite made her feel fulfilled. "I feel like no matter how much I do, it's never enough," she told me. "Anytime I just want to take a break, my body starts to freak out and get anxious. And so I keep working, because I'm comfortable being in my head. It's safer up here." She pointed to her head.

We worked on developing her custom self-soothing toolkit, which consisted of a blend of Eastern and Western healing modalities. In a few short months, she learned to talk to herself when she was stressed. When she noticed herself getting burned out, she reached into her toolkit for breath work, a walk around the neighborhood, and a tall glass of water before defaulting to burying her emotions in her work.

Start incorporating self-soothing practices and emotional regulation techniques to stay centered inside. This might include breathing exercises, gentle release with movement, sitting in silence, putting on your favorite pump-up song and having an impromptu dance party in your living room, giving yourself a big hug, or — my personal favorite — saying it out loud. As you observe your mind, begin by identifying your emotions. If being in your body is difficult for you, ask yourself out loud, "Where in my body am I feeling this?" As you embark on this journey of reconnecting with your body, be patient with yourself. If you've struggled with disassociation from your body, which is the state of disconnecting from one's thoughts, feelings, memories, or sense of identity, then at first you might struggle with connecting with your body. For a very long time in my own life, I felt disconnected from my body. Saying it out loud helped me make sense out of what was going on inside me. When I started incorporating breath work, movement, and other self-soothing techniques, like the ones mentioned below, I was able to bridge the gap between my mind, body, and creative spirit.

Use your words to express what your body cannot (yet). Trust that words are powerful enough to release emotions stored in your body. As you start speaking to yourself out loud with kindness and curiosity, your body will loosen up and speak back to you.

Vasavi's Top Three Self-Soothing Practices

- **Talk out loud to yourself the way you would with someone you love.** I suggest to all my clients that they keep a photo of themselves as a child on their fridge, on their desk, and taped to their bathroom mirror so they can practice speaking kindly to themselves when they are experiencing discomfort in their body. How would you speak to a young child or a friend who was going through a stressful situation? Comfort yourself as you would a child — and what better child than the one you used to be, who still lives inside you?
- **Wear something cozy and soft.** I mean, what's better when you're feeling sad than your favorite long-sleeve T-shirt, which has been broken in oh so perfectly, and your favorite soft sweatpants?
- **Immerse yourself in warm water.** I never used to be a person who took baths. But once I started, I

knew I had to incorporate it into my self-soothing practices. Whether you begin your morning with a warm bath or end your day with one, make it a peaceful and relaxing experience. Some of my favorite bath items include bath bombs, bath salts, essential oils to drop into the bathwater, and dried eucalyptus. Oh, and of course, a playlist that melts away any worries and stress.

Practice saying out loud how you feel as you partake in any of the above self-soothing practices. Many of my clients share that they hear thoughts like, "What's the point of even doing this?" In these moments, as you fill up the tub with water and get ready to immerse yourself, you can practice saying out loud, "This warm bath is going to feel so comforting. I want to feel relaxed, and this bath is going to help me slow my mind and breath down." Using your voice will help you come back to the present moment rather than getting sucked in by critical voices, memories of the past, or thoughts of the future.

Where Do Their Feelings End and Yours Begin?

Left unexpressed, your emotions will be hard to separate from those of another person. Said another way, you will have trouble setting and maintaining boundaries. Your emotions give you all the information you need in order to understand what you require to feel safe — emotionally, physically, and mentally. And if you struggle with expressing your boundaries, it's because you have yet to express your emotions to yourself out loud. When you express your emotions out loud to yourself and get curious about what's going on internally, what you will find is that the very thing you've been seeking from others, you can give to yourself. Matter of fact, you have to learn how to give yourself what you need, so that you can express those needs in other areas of life: work, relationships with friends and family, romantic partnerships.

But it can be very vulnerable to state your boundaries and needs out loud. How can you even begin to express your boundaries and needs to other people when you haven't taken the time to be vulnerable with yourself? By not acknowledging and expressing your feelings out loud to yourself, you continue to stay clogged. As long as you are focused on the story, plot, and characters, you can never evolve past the drama. You stay stuck in the "he/she/they said" loop and disturb your own peace. Focusing on the details keeps you from seeing the bigger picture, which is, "How is this impacting me right now?" or "How does this make me feel?" You need to give yourself the space to simply say out loud how you're feeling, without the fear of being shamed. When you say it out loud in real time, you are able to see beyond the minutiae and process uncomfortable feelings, thereby expanding your ability to be with any situation, regardless of how challenging it may be.

Boundaries Begin with You

Communicating your boundaries becomes a lot easier when you learn how to give yourself what you emotionally need in times of stress. For example, say you're feeling nervous about a big presentation you have to make at work, and you have only a few days to prepare for it. You feel pulled in all directions by family, friends, and coworkers — everyone seems to need you right this second. Check in with yourself by asking out loud, "What am I feeling?" or "Where in my body am I feeling this?" Breathe and respond truthfully: "I'm experiencing nervousness in my stomach. This presentation could determine whether I get promoted or not, and I just want to do a great job." Let that sink in. Then say to yourself, "It's totally understandable that you're nervous. This is a huge milestone in your career. I promise we will get through this together. What do you need when you're feeling nervous?" Then, pay attention. The voice inside that responds next may be the part of you that needs support with managing its energy and boundaries, so listen to what that part of you has to say. Perhaps this part of you says, "I feel like everyone needs me, and all I need is some space to practice my presentation, because I'm feeling overwhelmed." Great! Say that out loud. Now that part of you is opening up, and you can respond by saying, "What would space look like?"

Use the conversation with yourself to understand the boundaries you need to create in order to feel space as you get ready for your presentation. You can bring in your logical mind to help execute whatever solution you come up with. This is a beautiful illustration of how your mind and body can work together to create strategies that are integrated with your full self. Maybe you set up an autoresponder email or send a quick text to your clients, colleagues, friends, and family to let them know you're on a deadline, and voilà! You've just communicated your boundaries. Remember, it starts with you getting clear on how you're feeling and what you need in order to feel grounded. And be patient: parts of you that haven't been expressed will be slow to open up. The more you use a gentle and curious approach with yourself, the safer these parts will feel opening up and speaking to you.

There are many ways to soothe yourself, so listen to what that voice says back to you and then follow through and give yourself what you need. For example, maybe you hear that voice say, "What I need is to breathe and be told that I'm smart and I can do this!" You see what we just did? This dialogue is filled with kindness and encouragement, right? It also has a flavor of strength and motivation. This is how most of us talk to our loved ones. So why don't we talk to ourselves in this way?

When you express your feelings out loud and ask yourself questions that get you closer to what you need in those moments, you no longer become thrown off by having a normal human response. You can check in, talk out loud to yourself, ask curious questions, and become emotionally self-sufficient, rather than being at the mercy of your unspoken feelings. The next time you're in a situation that triggers you, turn inward. Ask your body what it is feeling. Don't keep your feelings bottled up inside. Express your emotions out loud.

After we become more fully in touch with our emotions, we become able to access our intuition. That's the next step of our work, which we'll learn about in chapter 6.

SAY IT OUT LOUD EXERCISE

Prompt: Notice when you tell, argue, package, or rationalize with your mind about how you're feeling. Observe when your attention drifts out of your body and up into your mind.

Practice: As you notice what is going on inside you, be mindful of your breathing. Put your right hand over your heart, close your eyes, and take a few deep breaths in and out. Ask yourself out loud, "What am I experiencing in this moment?" Pay attention, respond, and continue to dialogue with yourself as you start opening up. Listen to what you need — and then follow through on what you've discovered. For example, if what you need is to practice deep breathing and go for a walk, go do that. If you need to breathe and tell yourself you are safe, then take as many deep breaths as you require to calm your nervous system and then say out loud, "I am safe, and I am OK."

Promise: Promise yourself that no matter how big or intense the feeling that arises, you will be kind, empathetic, and patient with yourself. Commit to being patient instead of trying to rush through your feelings. Make it a regular practice to check in with yourself out loud by asking, with kindness, "What am I feeling in this moment?" The way to build trust and confidence in yourself is to ask for what you need, listen, and then put in the effort to give that to yourself. You are worth making the effort for, no matter how large or small the thing you need may be.

SAY IT OUT LOUD AFFIRMATIONS

I treat myself with the same love and kindness that I would give to a cherished friend.
It's healthy to feel my full range of emotions and express them freely.
I have a right to feel safe and have my feelings seen and heard by others.

Chapter 6

ASK YOUR INTUITION
OUT LOUD

Answer this out loud:
What causes you to doubt your gut feelings?

Every year, my family and I used to go to a Hindu summer retreat where Pujya Swami Dayananda Saraswati was the main guru. From an early age, I was enamored of the way he translated Hindu scriptures using his impeccable mastery of the English language and razor-sharp logic. Hundreds of minitexts were created from our scriptures and sold at the retreat bookstore. One summer, I came upon a book he wrote titled *Problem Is You, Solution Is You*. The thought that any problem I was having in life could be solved — and, even better, that *I* was the answer — was a new concept for me to grasp. I was hungry to become the solution in my own life.

It wasn't until much later that I realized every single situation I had been through — the good, the bad, the ugly — could have been avoided had I only listened to my intuition. Instead,

I listened to the inner voice that was consistently fueled by fear and to the voices of those around me, who were in no way qualified to help guide my life. I ignored my intuition because I thought those whispers were "crazy." I used to call myself paranoid when I had a gut feeling about something — but, sure enough, my intuition was always 100 percent spot-on.

In this chapter, you will learn how to communicate with your intuition by asking the right kinds of questions; stay open to the wisdom of your body; and discover everyday practices to help develop and strengthen your relationship with your intuition. This is your opportunity to calm the chaos, slow down, enjoy your inner silence, and strengthen your intuition. All *you* need to do is trust that all the answers you are seeking are right there and be willing to exercise patience with yourself.

When Did You Stop Trusting Yourself?

My nephew asks a lot of questions. That's how he learns. He asks questions, and he listens to the answers. If he has a follow-up question, he doesn't hesitate to ask that either. He doesn't worry about being "too much," and he doesn't give up until *he* feels complete with the conversation. What I find most fascinating is that he has the confidence to keep asking if he doesn't know the answer. If children have the purity of intention and trust to ask questions, believe what the adults have to say, and have no fear in asking for clarity, then why don't we have that same trust in ourselves as grown-ups?

Notice any thoughts that may sound like, "I'm not very intuitive," or "I suck at being silent," or "I can't be alone or with myself." Say these thoughts out loud, and pay attention to how it feels in your body when you do. Most likely, it doesn't feel good. And why would it? You're telling yourself that you've failed before you've even begun! Be open to shifting these thoughts to something like, "I am an open and clear channel to receive messages through my inner silence" or "My body is a powerful messenger, and I am open to receiving guidance." Say these newly reframed thoughts out loud. How does it feel to speak to yourself with trust and confidence? A bit weird at first? Or maybe by now you've relaxed a little. The first step to rebuild trust with yourself, your body, and your intuition is to be aware and notice what you're telling yourself about your ability to tap into that intuition. Stay open to different ways for you to reconnect with your intuition.

Inner Silence Is the Source of Your Intuition

The key to accessing your intuition when confronted with a problem, challenge, obstacle, or even a simple decision, such as "What do I want to do tonight?" is to connect with your *inner silence*. Getting quiet with yourself, your ideas, your creative process, and the depth of who you are is by far the greatest gift you can give yourself. We're always going to have something that demands our attention, something that feels way more urgent than the need for us to sit quietly with ourselves. It gets loud inside our heads, which is why connecting with nature, channeling your creativity, and consciously choosing to slow down will help you cultivate an internal part of you that is pure silence. This inner silence is the source of your intuition.

Stay Open to Your Inner Guidance

Your intuition will communicate with you through a feeling, a sense of knowing, a sound, even through taste! Be willing to be open, be patient, and trust that your intuition will speak to you. I want you to think about your entire being, including your mind, body, and spirit, as a channel through which your intuition moves. Every single practice in this book is intended to declutter your channel. Basically, for your intuition to speak to you, you need to unclog a lot of the gunk that's been blocking your channel. This gunk I am referring to consists of all the voices in your head that keep you stuck, in fear mode, and paralyzed with self-doubt and self-scrutiny. At some point in our lives, we disconnected from the truth within us. Talking to and responding to your intuition out loud essentially moves energy through you and out of you, thereby keeping your channel clean and free-flowing. It's a lot easier to be open to your inner guidance when you don't have excess energy in the form of thoughts, beliefs, and stories blocking the path.

Being open allows you to access your intuition, no matter how dark things get for you. When you notice that you're stuck or feeling heavy energy, you can start clearing your mind by saying out loud, "I notice that I'm feeling stuck right now." The act of acknowledging that you're feeling stuck — and saying it out loud — starts to move your energy because it's no longer *in* your body in the form of thoughts and feelings; it's now *out* of you, where you can hear it and respond with, "How can I help you? Talk to me, I am here for you." In that moment, you're not only releasing stuck energy from inside you, but you're also working toward a healing solution to feel better within yourself. Your responsibility is to be honest with yourself about everything. No more justifying, minimizing, or brushing aside. Acknowledge when you feel stuck. And focus on listening and staying open to receiving guidance from within.

Ask the Right Questions

Do you ever notice that when someone asks you a question that involves a yes or no response, the conversation doesn't really go anywhere significant? Unless the other person asks a follow-up question or you keep speaking beyond a yes or no, it's pretty much a dead-end dialogue. The same goes for how you speak to your intuition. The best types of questions are those that are emotionally neutral and open-ended. For example, "Am I going to get the job I applied for?" would be considered a yes or no question. Or "I'm a good person, right?" would be a rhetorical question, because you're looking for a particular answer that you already know. A better question to tap into your intuition might be, "How can I show up as my Higher Self in this moment?" or "What do I need to embrace / let go of?" Allow your intuition to speak to you and begin to dialogue with yourself.

Forcing or rushing answers isn't the way to be more connected to your intuition. Talking *at* yourself versus talking *to* yourself will produce two very different outcomes. When you talk at yourself, you'll most likely shut down, because who wants to be talked at? But when you talk to yourself, communicating with curiosity and openness, you can engage in a real conversation, one leading to more understanding about whatever situation you need guidance on. No matter what the scenario is, you can access the intuitive whispers within you. As time goes by, what were once whispers will become the loudest voices in your head. This is a *great* sign that you're becoming more in tune with your intuition.

> Let go of the struggle. Stop making things more difficult for yourself.

On December 25, 2021, I decided I was ready to let go of emotional weight that had manifested as a little extra cushion on my body. I had indulged during the holidays, as many of us do, and felt guilty and ashamed. I was done beating my body up for having an extra layer or two of flesh. For two hours I evaluated how I had been able to create so many wonderful things in my life yet still struggled with my body weight. I had come to a point where I felt heavy and unattractive. Maniacally shopping online for lacinato kale and green juice so I could starve my body and lose weight was no longer an option for me. Constantly trash-talking to my body in front of the mirror was no longer an option for me. Feeling helpless around my physical health was no longer going to be my go-to. I knew that my approach would have to be rooted in self-acceptance and fun.

I made a commitment to choose ease with my body out loud. I first admitted how I felt: "I feel heavy and unattractive." I then asked my body out loud, "What is really going on with us? Please talk to me." Through my dialogue with my body, I received the message loud and clear that I had been using food to mask how I felt in other areas of my life. My body spoke back to me and said, "It's time for us to feel light." That's all I needed to hear to set the tone for how I was going to approach feeling better in my body. Feeling lighter wasn't just about eating well; it also showed me where I was still carrying the emotional weight from my past.

Be open to receiving support in all forms. One of the most impactful actions I took was enlisting the help of a dear friend of mine who guided me through an entire process to help me reconnect with my body. (For a glimpse into what we did, listen to "Naked," the full *Say It Out Loud with Vasavi* podcast episode where I take you behind the scenes: https://www.vasavikumar .com/blog/ep3.)

My point in sharing this is to highlight the nature of intuition. Your intuition will never guide you upstream. It will always be the voice of ease. And, at times, you may be scared to listen to what your intuition says. At first you may think, "This feels too easy," and guess what? That's because the right answer, the one that is most aligned with the truest part of you, is the simplest one for your highest growth and evolution. Your intuition may at first be speaking to you quietly, but the more you turn inward and talk to yourself (out loud), the stronger the relationship you will have with your inner wisdom. Your intuition has never left you. You just stopped talking (and listening) to yourself! All it takes is you getting curious about *your* truth for your body to start responding to you. Whether you're looking to feel good in your body or to cultivate the confidence to go after an exciting opportunity, your intuition will speak to you through your body. Your job is to start the conversation, listen, and stay open to what it says.

What's something that comes effortlessly for you? What feels light and easy? Choose at least one area of your life where you feel confident, one that is a natural extension of your soul. That's what it feels like when you're tapped into your intuition. Maybe, like my sister, you can whip up a five-star dinner with just a few ingredients from the fridge. Perhaps you were born with the ability to connect with anyone and give rock-solid advice. Maybe you're the go-to person in your social group when it comes to event planning. Perhaps you have an eye for interior design and can put together home decor with ease. Every single one of us has something that comes naturally to us, something that just flows through and out of us when we decide to do it. What would it take to expand that feeling into other areas of your life? Imagine if every time you were confronted with a challenge, you tapped into the part of you that is cool as a cucumber and confident that what is meant for you will make its way into your life, no matter what. That is how your intuition will speak to you: with clarity, calmness, and confidence.

Move Beyond Your Meditation Pillow

I'll be the first to admit that I struggle with focusing. My brain moves quickly, which often makes it difficult for me to sit and meditate. However, once I started to incorporate practices, routines, and rituals that had nothing to do with sitting on a meditation pillow, I came to love sitting in silence and focusing on my breathing. All of these ways have allowed me to move my body, connect with nature, and channel my creativity. I have often found that my intuition speaks to me when I'm the most playful and open. That doesn't mean that your intuition won't speak to you if you're sad. In fact, you don't need to feel good to be in touch with your intuition. You just need to get out of your head and into your body and start feeling. Period.

I have some favorite *practical* ways to help you unplug, reconnect with yourself, and become more intentional about cultivating silence externally as a way to get in touch with your inner silence. See which ones resonate for you:

- Plan your tomorrow today. Instead of waking up frantically, not knowing what appointments, tasks, and projects you need to work on, start your day with clarity. When you start your day with clarity and minimize unnecessary chaos, it's easier to connect with your intuition.
- Upon awakening, say, "Thank you" out loud for being alive another day.
- Be your own morning motivation. Don't clutter your mind with the words of other people. Do this instead: record a five-minute pump-up audio or video of you motivating yourself.
- Try this: For twenty-four hours, refrain from listening to a single podcast (including mine), asking for any advice, watching motivational videos, reading self-help books, scrolling through Instagram for advice, reading your horoscope (guilty as charged), and doing anything else that involves you stepping

outside of yourself to get answers that you most likely already know. See what it feels like to be your biggest cheerleader, listen to your gut or intuition, use common sense, lean on your values and moral compass, and use your basic human consciousness to get through life and be (more than) OK.

- Drive in silence. Experiment with how you feel with music playing in the background versus being silently with your thoughts. You can also use the time in your car to work through any challenges you're experiencing, out loud.

- Use a text message autoresponder when you're driving. Here's an example of what my friends and family receive: "Vasavi is currently operating a moving vehicle. She will respond when she isn't driving. Have a blessed day!"

- Talk to yourself out loud (you know I had to add that one in, right?). Speak out loud the whispers that come to you when you're in silence. That's your intuition speaking.

- Set your phone on Do Not Disturb for short periods of time throughout your workday.

- Check emails only at designated times two to four times a day.

- Set up an autoresponder message to manage email response expectations.

- Block out creative time or quiet time in your calendar. Be intentional about spending quality time with yourself and your creative projects.

- Choose music that speaks to the quiet within you. When I'm working, I listen to smooth piano jazz. Find what soothes you.

- Do one thing at a time. We continue to stoke our inner chaos by juggling multiple tasks. Block out periods of time to focus on completing one task at a time.

- Say no to social gatherings, especially if the voice inside you is advising, "Just rest tonight. Spend some time with yourself."

- Say yes to social gatherings that feel outside of your comfort zone. You may experience thoughts like, "Am I good enough to hang out with these people?" or "No one is going to notice if I'm even there." If your intuition is saying, "This sounds like fun, and connection with others feels like just what I need," then go!

- Be mindful of how you speak to yourself throughout the day. Become acutely aware of every single thing you are thinking and saying to yourself.

- Take a break. You don't need to wait till you're mentally, physically, and emotionally burned out to give yourself the gift of rest.

- Be intentional about winding down for the evening so you can shut off your mind. If you notice that you tend to be attached to your work emails, for example, it's time to set a boundary with yourself.

- Listen to delta waves or relaxing music to put you to sleep.

- Put your phone in another room before you go to bed.

- If winding down and quieting your mind is difficult, especially at bedtime, make your environment conducive to rest by dimming the lights and putting away all electronics.

It takes time, compassion, and a high dosage of honesty to reconnect with aspects of yourself that you have abandoned. For a while, you may require seclusion. Solitude will disclose all the ways in which you've betrayed your intuition. In those moments of quiet when your intuition starts to speak to you, you can say out loud, "I'm here. Talk to me. You have my full attention." The more you hear your own voice out loud, the more you'll feel like you're coming closer to yourself.

No Shame in Asking for Help

When you live a life according to your intuition, you'll be surprised at how many doors open for you. Support that you didn't even know existed will present itself to you in a myriad of ways. But it's no mistake. When you listen to your intuition, you can never — and I repeat, *never* — make the wrong decision. The right people, places, and situations just seem to show up in your life. You're not required to do everything on your own. Far from it. Asking and tapping into your intuition requires you to surrender to *all* possibilities of support to help guide you throughout your journey. Support may come in the form of neighbors, therapists, strangers, a friend of a friend, or hired services like a personal chef, housekeeper, or assistant.

Be open to inviting in all possible solutions rather than insisting on being the sole provider. You do not exist on an island. If you pride yourself on being hyperindependent, this is a trauma response from a young age. You realized early in your childhood that you were safer relying on yourself than opening yourself up to potential letdowns from others. Be aware of the fact that support doesn't have to look a specific way. When you are guided by your intuition, you'll also be guided to support that shows up in different ways.

Think about all the times in your life when you felt that

something was off. Or when you ignored your intuition and relied on your mind to guide you. All those times you dismissed your intuition as being paranoid, didn't you say to yourself afterward, "I should have listened to my gut?" The problem is that we haven't learned how to distinguish our truth from all the other voices in our head. The solution is to speak our deepest thoughts out loud, reconnect with our bodies, and live an intuitively guided life.

> **Out of all the voices in your head, it takes courage to listen to the quietest one.**

Choosing to seek guidance from your intuition rather than anyone else around you is a *bold move*. It's a bold move because you have so many external options to choose from: blogs, podcasts, social media, TV, movies, books... the list goes on. It takes courage to say, "You know what? I'm going to listen to myself and do what feels right *for me*." You are intuitive. You've just been listening to all the other voices around you and in your head. At some point in your life, you disconnected from your intuition. You've been making decisions based on what outside forces say is "right" instead of what's right *for you*. And that's why listening to your intuition is a bold move. You're choosing to let go of what anyone else thinks about how you should live your life. You're choosing to do life on your terms. And that, my friend, is courageous.

Find a quiet, comfortable, cozy spot in your home or wherever you feel most grounded. Practice the Say It Out Loud exercise below either sitting upright or lying down, whichever feels most comfortable for you. You're being encouraged to feel what your body is saying and use your voice to prompt your intuition. Trust the wisdom of your body. Regardless of how your body responds, this is where you get to reparent yourself, grow spiritually and emotionally, and do what is best for your healing. You, the adult, get to step in and speak, listen, and respond to the child within you, telling them they are safe. And this is where you get to deepen the connection with yourself.

In the next chapter, we will talk about how feelings of resistance toward trusting your intuition can get in the way of growth. Your intuition — which comes from your heart — is often in tension with your ego, which sometimes demands that we ignore our intuition in the name of doing things we think we "should" be doing (like people-pleasing) or things that are unhealthy for us (such as using substances to escape from a reality that is in conflict with what our intuition needs). The resistant ego represents old patterns of unhealthy behaviors, while our intuition represents growth and peace.

SAY IT OUT LOUD EXERCISE

Prompt: Notice when you're feeling lost, confused, or stuck. Observe any frustration, anxiety, and/or impatience in your body. Listen to the internal conflict between what you "should" and "shouldn't" do.

Practice: Place your hands on your heart, stomach, or wherever feels most comfortable for you. Connect with your breath. Choose whichever of these questions resonate with you most strongly. Ask and respond to any or all of these questions out loud:

- "What is going on inside me?"
- "What answers am I seeking?"
- "Why do I feel lost, stuck, and confused?"
- "How can I improve this situation?"

- "What is the next best step to take regarding this situation?"
- "Is there something that I am missing or not seeing? If so, what is it?"
- "What is the problem for which I'm seeking a solution?"

Practice being a safe space for yourself and your intuition by speaking in a way that is gentle, curious, and tender. This may sound like you using a softer tone of voice, or maybe you feel safe with a steady and deep pitch with yourself. Take a deep breath and let your intuition speak through you. Continue to ask yourself questions and answer them out loud.

Promise: Promise to tap into your intuition first before seeking external guidance. When confronted with a challenging situation, difficult conversation, or internal conflict about what you "should" or "shouldn't" do, turn within first. Make a commitment to talk, listen, and respond to your intuition with nothing less than kindness and respect.

SAY IT OUT LOUD AFFIRMATIONS

There is no such thing as a wrong decision as long as I am listening to my intuition.
I give myself plenty of space and silence to let my intuition speak to me.
I trust myself to make the best decision for me.

Chapter 7

VOICE YOUR RESISTANCE OUT LOUD

Answer this out loud:
How do the negative voices in your head
keep you down?

Ever notice that whenever you experience a spark, the kind that makes you feel alive and makes you believe anything is possible, you're almost instantly confronted with...*that voice*? That's the voice of resistance. Resistance is the antimuse. It is the voice that will tell you you're selfish for taking time away from your kids to work on your book, or that you are an awful speaker and no one will understand you, or that you simply aren't smart enough to courageously pursue those dreams of yours.

We all experience resistance every single day, especially when trying to do something that will help us grow, such as exercising, investing in coaches, therapists, and other professionals to support our growth, or working on a creative project. You know that voice all too well. That voice that creeps up just as you're about to sit down to focus on your creative work or start a project that matters to your soul. That voice that might say, "Oh, this can wait. I have other things I must take care of," or "I don't have time, I have so much on my plate," or "This isn't perfect enough yet, so I can't share it with the world." That voice that convinces you everything else you're doing is way more important than the thing you most need to focus on.

Every time I sit down to write, my mind immediately tells me I "have to" check emails, voicemails, and texts. There is always something that absolutely needs my attention. Or my voices of resistance will be in the background while I work: "No one is going to understand what you're trying to say." Left to congregate in our minds, the voices of resistance can feel real and valid. Most of us don't want to dive deep into why we procrastinate on things we know we should be doing, resist taking action on our dreams, and self-sabotage — until we're finally fed up with ourselves or, worse, we're on our deathbed. Sometimes it's too late to change things, and that's just the reality. It's not too late for you, though. If you're working against yourself, it's time to learn how to move through your resistance, so that you can finish that piece of artwork, write that book, start that podcast, take that class, or do whatever has been speaking to your soul.

Give Your Resistance a Voice

Recall a time when all you needed was someone to give you compassion and understanding but instead were met with silence and invalidation. Maybe you struggled with certain subjects in school, and the only explanation given on your report card was, "Hyperactive and needs to learn how to focus." Or maybe you started a new position at work and were eager to do a great job, but when you sheepishly asked your boss, "I'm struggling with this — can you help me understand it?" you were dismissed or made to feel stupid. If every time you came up against an obstacle in the past, you didn't have anyone to gently guide you, now anytime you experience resistance, you freeze, procrastinate, or use other strategies to protect yourself from failure and humiliation.

Every single occurrence in our life that didn't have the space to be processed manifests as resistance. You can easily loosen the energy of your resistance by giving it a voice. Rather than getting angry with yourself and continuing to perpetuate the narrative of "I can't..." or "I don't have time...," notice when thoughts of resistance creep up, and get curious about what's driving your resistance. Say out loud, "I'm noticing resistance in my body." Give yourself the space to just breathe in and out. Then ask yourself out loud, "If my resistance had a voice, what would it say?" Once again, just be patient and breathe. From there, let your resistance speak to you. Maybe it says, "You're not smart enough to even do this. Why are you wasting your time?" This is where you get to be motivating, determined, and compassionate with yourself by saying out loud, "I'm good at this, and I'm going to keep moving forward, no matter what." Think about what you would say to a friend who was sharing their frustration about being stuck. Say that to yourself! The next time you hear the voice of resistance, see it for the lie that it is, say it out loud, and give yourself a much-needed pep talk to help you move through it. Your life is way too precious to not complete your mission on this planet.

Release Your Resistance

When I was nine years old, my mother put me in classical Indian singing classes with a teacher who was well-known in the South Asian community. She had a strong voice and an even harsher tongue. Every time my mother would take me to class, I felt like I was going to throw up. And because I was so terrified of my teacher, I rarely felt motivated to practice my singing homework. One day during our weekly music classes, which took place in the basement of my teacher's house, she was teaching me a new song, and I struggled to pick up the nuances of the melody. My teacher slammed the book down, raised her voice, and said something to me that I can't remember, but even to this day I recall how I felt. Her volume, tone, and anger scared the heck out of me. I looked down, with tears about to roll down my face, and quietly walked upstairs.

My mother, who usually wasn't afraid to stand up to anyone, didn't say anything to my music teacher, even though she had heard everything. But maybe if she had stood up for me, the voice of my music teacher wouldn't have been so loud. In that moment what I needed the most was someone to show me that I did not deserve to be treated in such an aggressive way. As a teenager and even well into my twenties, I resisted sitting down and practicing music. As I got older, my resistance to practice bled into other areas of my life: I would half-ass things or try to find shortcuts. I associated practice with getting yelled at or doing something wrong. It wasn't until I started to voice my own resistance and say out loud, "I'm afraid of messing up and making a mistake" that I was able to free myself from resistance to practice and discipline.

No matter how hard we try to block out painful memories, the feeling of that memory resides in our body. In an instant, our nervous system can be triggered, and we can be brought back to a memory, most likely the initial event that conditioned our nervous system to live in a constant state of "something bad is about to happen." Speaking harshly to yourself only makes you rebel against yourself. When's the last time telling yourself that you sucked at something actually motivated you for a consistent length of time? In some cases, maybe when you speak harshly, it motivates you, but try to not just have one approach with yourself. In moments when you notice your resistance, be willing to challenge it to see how much more compassion you can show toward yourself.

For example, when you hear thoughts like, "You suck at this...," instead of giving up, pause, take a deep breath in, exhale out, and say out loud, "That's not helpful. I'm doing the best that I can right now." There will also be times where the voice of your resistance will convince you that you're crazy for pursuing an idea, and you may hear, "Who do you think you are, trying to do this?" In those moments, instead of tossing your hands up in the air and throwing yourself a pity party, you can say out loud, "I'm not going to entertain you right now." Nip it in the bud.

When you hear the voice of your resistance, rather than taking it to heart, picture this: your resistance is the creative child inside you that got silenced and shamed along the way by your inner cynic who is beyond condescending and is just terrified of failing. That voice is not yours. It does not belong to you. You most likely picked it up from a teacher, friend, colleague, parent, sibling — the list can go on and on. But ultimately it is your responsibility to voice that resistance out loud and work through your inner dialogue out loud.

> **Resistance will tell you that you've failed before you even start. Giving a voice to it diminishes its power over you.**

Your resistance will present itself in a variety of ways as an initial or continuous response to you sitting down and focusing on your most important objectives and goals, including the urge to delay the process of starting. You see, what happened when I was a kid taking music classes had an impact on how I viewed practice and discipline. I often avoided doing the necessary work to prepare myself because I was so afraid of messing up. And maybe you're like this too. Maybe when it comes to being there for other people, you're right on top of it. You're excellent at helping others pursue their dreams, or you're a natural-born leader and can guide others to simple solutions. But when it comes to yourself, you hesitate, procrastinate, and resist doing the things that you know would move you closer to your dreams. Maybe you get joy out of trying new ways to express your creativity but resist doing it. Our stories don't need to be the same for resistance to be the thread that binds us together. If you're human, you experience resistance.

Every part of you needs to be addressed, heard, and integrated for you to show up in your entirety as a creative, expressive soul. The solution to working through resistance is threefold: noticing it, responding to it out loud, and taking inspired action. By voicing your resistance out loud, you meet yourself exactly where you are while reminding yourself of what your commitments are and who you're becoming through this process. It's where the magic happens.

> **Resist the urge to allow resistance to stop you in your tracks.**

To notice resistance, respond to it, and take action in spite of it are three very different but interconnected experiences. I want to walk you through all three to prepare you for the Say It Out Loud exercise at the end of the chapter.

Notice Resistance

When I was a kid, I would tell my father, "I feel like I have a camera on my shoulder that's watching me." Only much later in my life did I learn that what I was talking about was my conscious-ness, or my observing self. In the Hindu scriptures we refer to this consciousness or awareness as Brahman. The experience feels as if you have floated out of your body and are watching yourself in a movie.

As you're noticing resistance, observe how your mind speaks to you. All I want you to experience here is the space between you and *you* — you the human and *you* the consciousness. That's it. Notice how resistance feels in your body. Notice if you judge. Simply pay attention to what your resistance is saying to you. Do you hear voices saying things like, "Ugh, I don't want to do this," or "I'll just start later"?

Before I continue onto the next two steps for dealing with resistance, here is a gentle reminder that we are all made up of many parts. You may want to silence parts of you because you're ashamed of them. Stop. Get intimate with every single part of you on your journey to becoming fully integrated.

Respond to Resistance

Have you ever noticed how easily you respond with solid-as-a-rock advice when your friends come to you in distress? Whether they're beating themselves up, judging themselves for whatever flaw they perceive as catastrophic, or overthinking, *you* always manage to respond with compassionate and sound advice. That's because you aren't emotionally attached to their story, so you can tap into the logical part of your mind and give a simple solution to help them move through their resistance. Your tone may be firm, but they know that you genuinely care about their well-being, and that's why they value you as a friend — for your gentle firmness.

Gentle firmness looks, feels, and sounds like you are being the kind but no-nonsense friend I just described. Let's return to the example above, the voice that says, "Ugh, I don't want to do this," or "I'll just start later." Responding to resistance here might sound like, "[Insert your first name], I know you're resisting this right now, but let's get to work." Play with the gentle firmness approach and have fun finding fresh ways of communicating with yourself. Maybe you are the highly energetic cheerleader type, and saying out loud, "You got this! You are a warrior and were born for this!" will help you move through your resistance. Or maybe you are the motivating coach that you've been looking for, who would say, "Stop wasting time. This is your one life — make something of it." Find the voice that gets you to move through your resistance, and keep using it.

The more you hear yourself speak and respond to your resistance out loud, the more you will be able to distinguish between the voice of resistance that is saying, "I don't want to do this" and the voice of reason that is saying, "Let's take a break so we can reenergize." It's important to know the difference between resistance and reason, because the truth is, some days are going to be more difficult than others! You may experience more resistance on some days for a multitude of reasons. In those moments, the last thing you need to be doing is being harsh with yourself. Gentle firmness? Yes. Harshness? No. This is where you need to honor the ebb and flow of your creative process. Understand that even though you may hear a voice that sounds like resistance, it could also be the part of you that yearns to feel creatively energized and needs to get out in nature to gain some inspiration before getting back to the thing you were working on. When it comes to your resistance, you're learning how to talk to yourself so that you are taking consistent action toward your dreams. Find out what that voice sounds like. When you do, you will no longer get in your own way — because now, you know how to break down the wall of resistance within yourself.

Take Action in Spite of Resistance

There are so many things we want to do. So many things we have dreamed of doing. So many things we want to say. Yet when our resistance to doing the thing takes over, we miss out on the opportunity to give ourselves a real shot at this thing called life. Every time you let your resistance win — which manifests as you not taking action or doing the hard or scary thing — the belief that has limited you up until this point stays intact. The narrative you've been telling yourself continues to run your life. Resist the urge to let your resistance stunt your growth. Voice your resistance out loud.

Noticing and responding to resistance with gentle firmness inevitably results in taking action in spite of the resistance. All three experiences together help move you closer to your goals and true self. On the other side of resistance is freedom — the freedom to be you, ALL of you. The you who has power to move through your most deeply ingrained beliefs. The you who has the courage to flow from ideation to creation.

Once you learn how to talk to your resistance, voice it out loud, and soften its wall, you can go even further and begin to explore the other parts of you that you have hidden. Your ego wants these parts of you to stay hidden, to protect you from shame or fear, but it is time to bring your true self into the light. And you do this by owning your flaws. This is the work we will do in the next chapter.

SAY IT OUT LOUD EXERCISE

Prompt: Notice when you experience resistance, typically right before doing the hard thing (creative project, difficult conversation, unpleasant interaction, or expressing how you feel). Observe your thoughts, feelings, and body responses when you're in resistance.

Practice: Using the voice of gentle firmness, ask the questions below to open the door for dialogue with yourself. Go through each of these questions and answer out loud to express what comes up. Trust that all the answers are inside you. Pay attention to them and let them move through you and out of you.

- "What am I resisting?"
- "What am I unwilling to let go of here?"
- "Where in my body do I feel this resistance?"
- "What action am I avoiding taking right now?"
- "Whose voice is this?" (Teacher, partner, family member, friend?)
- "What would I do differently if I felt safe to move forward?"
- "Hey, [insert your name], I'm here for you. Share with me what's going on inside you."

Promise: Promise to create the space to say out loud what you're experiencing whenever you notice you are in resistance. Your resistance shows you where to practice gentle firmness with yourself. Be the encouraging voice of a coach who helps you get through the tough times when all you want to do is give up on yourself or when you just need a no-BS reality check.

SAY IT OUT LOUD AFFIRMATIONS

When I set my mind to something, nothing and no one can stop me.

I can be both gentle and firm with myself when I want to give up.

I replace the voice of impossibility with the voice of encouragement.

Chapter 8

OWN YOUR FLAWS OUT LOUD

Answer this out loud:
What parts of yourself do you judge the most?

In the final rap battle scene of the movie *8 Mile*, B-Rabbit (played by rapper Eminem) is up against his opponent, Papa Doc (Anthony Mackie). B-Rabbit has spent the entire movie being beaten up, tortured, and ridiculed for being "white trash" and living in a trailer with his alcoholic mother. But in the very last scene of *8 Mile*, B-Rabbit raps out loud every single one of his "flaws" and ends with, "Don't ever try to judge me, dude, / You don't know what the f*ck I've been through." Papa Doc is left standing speechless and surrenders. B-Rabbit wins the rap battle, rightfully so.

That scene is the best way for me to convey the inner strength and confidence that you build when you can say out loud, "This is who I am, flaws and all. And despite them all, I accept myself." In this chapter, you will begin to shift how you perceive your flaws and learn how to own the parts of yourself that you have typically tried to cover up. Simply stated, it's time to put aside your shame and own your flaws. Building confidence, and being openhearted with yourself and others, begins with acknowledging the very human aspects of who you are.

The Irony of Self-Judgment

The things we most commonly consider flaws and refrain from sharing with others are issues from our past, fears, secrets, and problems we're currently facing that we are embarrassed of. The irony is that as human beings, one of the things we desire most is to have deep, fulfilling relationships, but we think that to have these relationships we need to get people to like us. To get people to like us, we tell ourselves that our imperfections can't be shared with others. For example, have you ever gone through a tough financial period, and instead of being honest about that with your friends when they invite you out to dinner, you simply avoid their invitation? You assume that they will judge your current financial situation. Or, because you don't want to lose the friendship, you go to dinner anyway, even though you keep promising yourself to get on a budget.

This is where the irony comes in. All you want are deep, fulfilling, and honest relationships, but continuing to judge yourself will further distance you from your relationships. If you want people to truly see all of you, then you need to start by accepting every single part of you, especially the parts of yourself that you judge. In this instance, owning your financial situation out loud might sound like, "Right now, it isn't fiscally responsible for me to be spending money on going out to dinner." Own your reality and know that this isn't forever. Your financial situation can and will change.

The bigger point here is to own your current reality, whatever it is, and say it out loud to yourself. When you own it to yourself, it becomes a lot easier to own it out loud with others. Your perception of what other people will think of you for having certain imperfections is rooted in being judged for them in the past, but it's also the product of the voice in your head that continues to judge you. This is why owning your flaws out loud is powerful. My hope is that the judgmental voice in your head won't have as much power over you when you say it out loud, because once you hear how you're speaking to yourself internally, you will choose to be more accepting of your flaws.

As adults, we need to break out of the thinking that we are back in school and a teacher is grading us. Take what you were told in school with a grain of salt. Or maybe in college you had a professor who told you that you're a terrible writer. Or, later, a romantic partner who said that you are too needy and emotional. The parts of you that you think are flawed are all parts of who you are as a human being. There is only one of you walking this planet. Why would you ever want to condemn *any* part of you? And while I am all for you growing, learning, and transforming, I want you to trust the slow unraveling and reweaving process of becoming who you are as you uncover your insecurities and learn to speak to yourself with kindness and respect. The gold includes *all* the nuances of saying it out loud. Your flaws are just pieces of the authentic creation that you are becoming.

Understanding Your Flaws

Do you dislike the part of you that tends to overthink till you get exhausted? Great! Instead of judging it, how about seeking to understand this part of you by asking yourself out loud: "What does this part of me need to feel safe in this moment?" Or do you wish you weren't so clumsy that you fall over your own feet? Seek to understand this part of you. Own your clumsiness and say out loud: "Sometimes I can be clumsy. In fact, I can trip over my own feet!" If owning your flaws is brand-new to you and feels uncomfortable, perfect! Acceptance of every single part of you is an audacious move. Own that flaw out loud and say, "Owning my flaws is kind of hard for me because I'm embarrassed by them, and that gets in the way of me accepting them." The more you try to argue against your flaws, the harder it's going to be to connect not only with yourself but with other people. How can you deepen intimacy within yourself if you are unwilling to own the parts of you that make you you? Instead of judging your flaws, start to see them through a different lens.

Let's look at one of the most common reasons people give as to why they haven't started or completed their goals: procrastination. Now, if you've ever thought or said out loud, "I'm such a procrastinator," then listen up. And if you don't identify with the tendency to procrastinate, fill in the blank with whatever negative thing it is you say about yourself. In the example of procrastination, when you wait until the last minute to complete something, you get that energy boost that seemed to be missing earlier in the process. You're forced to focus on the task at hand. Suddenly, writing emails, responding to texts and voicemails, and checking social media no longer seem relevant or urgent. If you look at it that way, procrastination seems beneficial, doesn't it? The only time it becomes a flaw is when you judge it and attach a story to it. When you remove the judgment around it, it doesn't have that much power over you.

If you want to change something about yourself, like procrastination, then start by asking out loud, "Is this helping me or hurting me?" And if you can get honest about that, with curiosity and acceptance, you can have an eye-opening conversation with yourself. The part of you that procrastinates might say back to you, "This is my way of processing my creative ideas internally before I sit down to work." Having this kind of dialogue with yourself helps you understand your behaviors with compassion. And by having compassion toward yourself, you can stop beating yourself up, own this flaw of yours, and decide whether it is something you would like to change or keep.

Pay close attention to how you feel and what happens to your energy when you say your perceived flaw out loud. Identifying with this flaw — saying, "I am a procrastinator" — probably doesn't feel good, does it? Even if there is truth in it, every time you collapse your value, self-worth, and identity together with your flaws, you box yourself into an identity that feels unchangeable. But when you begin to choose how you speak to yourself about your flaws, you open your mind and heart to seeing yourself through a fresh perspective.

Notice Where You Withhold Acceptance

Notice when you judge your flaws or whether you get defensive when they are pointed out. Say out loud, "I'm noticing myself getting defensive about my flaws." Even pausing slightly to notice your need to defend yourself, and saying that out loud, begins to foster a dialogue of curiosity with yourself. When you notice yourself becoming defensive, say that out loud, and then allow the part of you that feels the need to defend your flaw to speak up. This is where you get to soften and practice being in vulnerability by saying out loud, "I'm afraid that if people see my flaws, then they won't love me anymore." This is a gentle process of allowing the most vulnerable parts of you to open up. If you struggle with owning your flaws, it may be because you have the experience of being judged for them. But remember this: just because you have flaws (like everyone!) doesn't make you any less worthy of acceptance and compassion.

Let's say you've been told time and time again that you aren't a very good listener and that you have a tendency to interrupt people. This may be very difficult for you to hear and own out loud, especially if you have placed an immense amount of pressure on yourself to be "perfect" at all costs. So rather than being able to own your flaws out loud, you feel extreme shame when your flaws are pointed out to you. This is where you get to practice honesty and curiosity with yourself. Rather than brush the feedback aside or be ashamed of your flaws, ask yourself out loud, "Is there any truth to this?" If you find it difficult to own your flaws in that moment, then gently say to yourself, "I love and accept you, no matter what, flaws and all. I'm not here to judge you. I want to understand you."

Every part of you is worthy of your love, tenderness, and acceptance, not just the parts that are "appropriate" and "acceptable" for the world to see. Your flaws are sensitive to disapproval and judgment. So to build your ownership of and confidence about your flaws, you need to let that part of you know that it is still loved in spite of its flaws. Importantly, instead of seeking that love externally, *you* are giving yourself that acceptance. Shifting from "I don't like this about myself" to "I tend to [fill in the blank], and I'm willing to understand myself and why I behave the way I do" will exponentially transform the conversation and relationship you're having with yourself about your flaws. To be able to walk into a room and feel confident in your skin requires you to know, understand, and embrace even the tiniest flaws that you have. And what if it is these very flaws that make you so lovable?

Reframing Your Flaws

Isn't it ironic how the words that people say to us can stay with us until we decide we no longer want to identify with them? Someone once told me that I had a "one-track mind." The way they said it made me think that there was something wrong with me. This comment stayed with me for most of my thirties. When I get lost in my creative work, I can tune everyone out. I felt selfish having a one-track mind. I saw my one-track mind as something that meant I was too busy to be bothered with other people. At least that's how my mind interpreted the label. When I started to reframe my perception of my one-track-mindedness and to appreciate that part of me, I stopped letting everything around me distract me, including the need to respond to texts immediately and to check social media to see who had messaged me. As it turns out, my one-track mind has allowed me to finish huge projects and other creative pursuits that I focus on, all because I lean into my perceived flaws.

Accepting your flaws will feel like being at the airport waiting to board your flight and hearing the dreaded announcement: "Due to inclement weather, this flight has now been delayed." There's not much you can do about it. Sure, you can argue with the airline representative, or you can complain to the people around you about how much it sucks, both of which are very normal human responses. However, arguing and complaining, while they may release some of your frustration, don't get you on the plane more quickly. The best way to deal with your flaws is just how you might want to respond to a delayed flight: "Well, I can fight the reality of this, or I can make the best of the situation." This attitude will free you up from resisting reality. Your flaws are a part of you. You can either spend your time and energy resisting them, defending them, or wishing they were different, or you can accept the reality of them and make the best out of who you are.

Reframing and accepting your flaws can sound like you saying, "This flaw is a part of me, and I am willing to understand and accept this part of me." I know that's easier said than done.

But you'll find that saying that out loud transforms any judgmental energy you have into loving compassion toward yourself. And even if you find yourself resistant to accepting your flaws, just know that this *is* the work. The work of noticing your pride, your unwillingness to accept yourself, is where you get to meet yourself with even more compassion and acceptance.

> **The key to being confident is to accept and own your flaws.**

My relationship to my body has been one of celebration and condemnation throughout the years. By my early twenties, I had gained 40 pounds as a result of the cocktail of mood stabilizers I was prescribed. Every day I would stand in front of the mirror and pinch my fat rolls, telling myself how unattractive I was. So I set out to lose the 40 pounds. I hired a nutritionist, joined a women's boot camp, and became obsessed with counting calories. I was the most disciplined I had ever been in my entire life. And I did it. I lost the 40 pounds. By the time my wedding rolled around, I was 129 pounds, slim, trim, and feeling better than ever. Then, after I got married, I moved to Kansas with my husband. I remember my nutritionist telling me, "Don't put too much pressure on yourself to keep your weight off. You're going through a lot of new transitions. You're moving, married, and starting a new life." I didn't think much of her advice, but sure enough, I gained back 20 pounds within two years of being married.

I used to think that with hard work, hustle, and ambition, I could get anything I wanted. And for the most part, I was right. I had the strength and power to make just about anything happen. But if I'm being completely honest, I didn't have any fun throughout my weight loss process. Sure, I learned how to eat healthily and found fun ways to move my body, but the mindset and energy that I was bringing into my journey said, "There is something wrong with me and my body, and in order for me to feel good about myself, I need to fix it." I was trying to erase what I perceived to be my flaw — my body size. And I was able to "fix" it temporarily. But eventually, my inner world caught up with my outer world.

Being motivated by your biggest insecurities can set you on a path to achieving your goals, to make yourself better. There's no denying that. But what is the point of hitting your goals if you've judged yourself throughout the process? Sure, you'll achieve your intention, but at what cost? To have the motivation to start and finish your goals, you need to accept who you are in this moment. You need to have an energy of enthusiasm and passion that surpasses the need to "fix" something about you. If you want to start your side business, do it because you have a passion for the thing that you're doing, not because you hate your day job. Your enthusiasm and passion will take you much farther in life than resentment and disapproval will. How you feel on the inside and who you become en route to your desired destination are just as important as, if not more important than, reaching the goal itself.

> **Owning your flaws creates a space of acceptance.**

Think about someone in your life whom you absolutely adore. I'm guessing that when you are around this person, you don't sit and scrutinize their every flaw, do you? You love them in the fullness of their humanity. Despite their flaws, you still treat them with the utmost love and respect, don't you? In fact, you probably love them *more* because of their flaws. Well, you are worthy of the same love and respect. Have the audacity to love and embrace all the parts of you. Despite what the media portrays as "beautiful," remember that you have the power to re-invent the relationship you have with your body, mind, and spirit. When you start to accept your flaws, you stop looking to other people to accept you, because you accept yourself. Don't underestimate the potency of embracing every single part of you.

Owning your flaws will give you a sense of inner freedom that you simply cannot get from the outside world. No matter how much someone tells you that they're proud of you, or love you, or cherish you, at the end of the day, if you do not accept every single part of you, you will always feel disconnected from the beauty of the present moment. When you begin to own your flaws out loud, that is next-level confidence. And when you do that, you create space for other people to be themselves around you.

Beyond your imperfections, you may be hiding a variety of other parts of you, such as your quirks, idiosyncrasies, and the other things that make you you! To explore these other, less expressed parts, playfully identify them, and express them out loud, we will draw on the childlike, inquisitive side of you in the following chapter.

SAY IT OUT LOUD EXERCISE

Prompt: Notice where you get defensive when something is pointed out about you. Observe how you speak to yourself when you bump up against one of your flaws. Pay attention to the things that you criticize and judge about yourself, in private or with others.

Practice: Ask and answer out loud, "Which of my flaws am I trying to defend/protect?" or "What part of myself am I trying to protect from being found out?" This is where you get to shift your perspective on your flaws. Tap into the part of you that is compassionate and understanding. Embody that part of you when you're owning your flaws out loud. Learn to love your flaws. Stop hiding them. You get to own that you have these flaws, and you also get to accept that they are just another part of you. Practice being curious about your flaws, just as you would be with a friend.

Promise: Promise to be curious and open-minded about your flaws. Commit to seeing them as unique characteristics of the different parts of you. Promise to be gentle with yourself as you embrace your flaws.

SAY IT OUT LOUD AFFIRMATIONS

I am worthy of treating myself with love and respect no matter what I have said or done.
Every part of me is deserving of my acceptance and love.
I am giving myself the gift of total acceptance.

Chapter 9

PLAY HIDE-AND-SEEK
OUT LOUD

Answer this out loud:
What parts of you have been in hiding
and waiting to be expressed?

Every year, my elementary school ran a writing contest called Reflections. The entire school received a writing prompt, and one student per grade was chosen as the winner. The year that I won, the writing prompt was "Does the sky have a limit?" I wrote, "The sky only has a limit if you believe it has a limit." My name being announced over the PA system as the winner of my grade was something I will never forget, for two reasons. First, I remember feeling so *alive* that day for being recognized for my creative writing abilities. Second, I remember what my classmate said as soon as I won: "Oh, so you think you're better than all of us now?"

From that day forward, I decided never to be *too* smart, bright, confident, intelligent, or happy. Instead, I chose to fly just under the radar. What happened that day created a story in my mind that said I would be met with disapproval, rejection, and social annihilation as soon as I succeeded. I took my potential for granted for most of my young adult life. I didn't push myself as much as I could have. I spent way too much of my time and energy cleaning up friendship squabbles and running after relationships that I thought would make me feel that same sense of aliveness I had felt in the second grade, only to end up disappointed and emotionally exhausted.

Most people are not afraid of failure, rejection, or humiliation. Most people are afraid of their own power. They are afraid of truly allowing their creative genius to be seen and heard. They're afraid of leaving behind their friends and family who aren't actively pursuing their goals and dreams. And, mostly, they are afraid of whom they can become if they truly allow *all* the parts of themselves to stop hiding and come out and play.

The impact of hiding parts of yourself is the ever-growing distance between the you that you show others and the you that you experience when you are alone with yourself. You've become a stranger to yourself and can't keep up with all the different versions of you that you outwardly portray. You will continue to feel like a stranger to yourself until you are willing to create the space for all the parts of you to be witnessed and acknowledged out loud. You will always have a sense that something is missing when you allow only some parts of you to be seen.

All the things you think are unacceptable, unlovable, and unworthy about you are the parts that need to be given a voice out loud. Speaking in a new way to the parts of yourself that you've hidden and judged will gently guide you toward showing up as your most authentic self in any situation. Instead of shutting down or watering down your responses to people, you'll express how you really feel, even though it would seem easier to hide your truth. Rather than keeping your mouth shut because you're afraid of coming off as pushy about that promotion at work, you will communicate your value and worth to your boss. Instead of replying, "Oh, it's fine, no problem" when someone crosses your boundaries, you will describe exactly how you feel and what your boundaries are. You will be straightforward and truthful. No drama. No resentment.

You have silenced and closeted some parts of you because you believed that these parts were somehow unacceptable or unlovable. These hidden parts are dormant and need a playful and creative outlet to express themselves. Consider this your permission slip to shine as brightly as possible and embrace all the parts of you. The key to creating space for your hidden parts to come out is to foster a conversation that is rooted in playful curiosity, just as you would when teaching something new to a child for the first time. In this chapter, you'll learn how to talk to the hidden parts of yourself by being playful and curious. When you do so, these hidden parts will reveal how they wish to channel themselves through various creative outlets. The extent to which your hidden parts reveal themselves to you and become comfortable and safe talking to you is determined by how you choose to engage in conversation with them, out loud.

Your Hidden Parts Are Your Superpowers

Which parts of yourself do you often hide? How is that impacting your relationships? When you feel unclear about something, do you tend to avoid and hide? Or do you confront the issue head-on and nip that lack of clarity in the bud? For Eliza, her most recent business partnership was starting to feel unclear and icky, and she knew that if she didn't at least send an email communicating her specific requests, the partnership would no longer be a viable one.

The part of herself that she often hid from others was what she labeled as her "pickiness." Her commitment to excellence in everything she does, which she had judged as being "picky," was holding her back from getting to the next level of her business. Her inner dialogue about this "picky" part of herself kept her from having difficult conversations because she didn't want to be judged for her "pickiness," and therefore she struggled with communicating her preferences, boundaries, and values. Sound familiar?

Eliza and I discussed how she would write an email to her partner. (It's worth mentioning here that saying it out loud isn't just helpful for vocally communicating. Saying it out loud will help you communicate through any channel, including writing, in the most authentic way possible.) I took Eliza through a three-step process that ultimately led to the most honest, direct, and clear email she had ever written. Use this process for yourself next time you need to communicate through email.

1. Say how you feel out loud, completely unfiltered. Use all the curse words; be as mean, angry, and annoyed as you want. Get it all out of you. Don't judge how you feel or how you're saying it. Raise your voice. Say exactly what you would say if there were no consequences. Do this in the privacy of your own space.

2. Say it out loud again. Be patient throughout this second step, because you may get frustrated and just want to get over it. Stop trying to get over it and start allowing thoughts and emotions to move through you. Acknowledge exactly how you feel. Repeat this step as many times as you must until you no longer feel an energetic charge or strong emotion.

3. Now, write your email from a calm, open, and grounded state of being. Read it out loud to yourself. Pay attention

to how you feel as you read each word out loud. You may feel uncomfortable because this is your first time being clear, direct, and honest. Or maybe you will feel elated that you're finally expressing yourself! Whatever feelings you have, just notice them. Remember, just because you feel a certain way or something is new or uncomfortable doesn't mean you shouldn't follow through. Send that email.

Eliza worked through this process with me and wrote an email that clearly expressed her feelings and her requests, something she never thought she could do. Her business partner replied, open to her suggestions and requests. And, for the record, Eliza's "pickiness" resulted in her product going from being sold at farmers' markets to being stocked in grocery stores across the state.

You get to choose how you relate to the hidden parts of yourself. You can call yourself a procrastinator, too much, too loud, quiet, shy, and whatever else you've been telling yourself that you are and shouldn't be. Or you can start to see those parts of you as your superpowers. Being quiet is your superpower. You've become an excellent listener because of it. Being too much is your superpower. Your energy can instantly lift the vibe of any room you walk into. Being committed to excellence is your superpower. You have an eye for detail and accuracy. Being empathetic is your superpower. You feel deeply for others and can understand anyone's situation.

Don't let society, media, religion, family, and the thoughts in your head keep you from seeing yourself through the eyes of curiosity and acceptance. Take time to understand the parts of yourself that you've hidden and the impact that hiding those parts has had in every area of your life. Don't let your hidden parts keep you from bringing your whole self to any situation.

Before you communicate with others, whether in person, via email, or over the phone, say out loud how you feel to yourself. Get clear with yourself first. Seek understanding of yourself first and let go of the expectation that others will understand you. The things that you've been hiding are your superpowers.

Come out, come out, whoever you are.

What would people discover about you if they could see all of you? Would they observe that you say things you don't mean, tell half-truths, or engage in complete lies? Would they see past the hard exterior you present to the world, only to find out that a part of you is soft and sensitive? Or would they find out that even though you present a prim and proper self to the external world, a part of you is completely unhinged and out of control? The parts of you that you've kept tucked away are just as valuable as the parts of you that you lead with. We need all the parts of you to be fully integrated for you to show up as the powerful being and creator that you were born to be.

One way to observe when you're hiding a part of yourself is to pay attention to whether your body posture expands or constricts. Notice when you feel like you're wearing a heavy cloak and are hunched over and when you feel expansive, with your chest open and shoulders back. Our bodies respond to how we feel internally. If you walk into a room and feel out of place, then naturally you will want to hide, and your body will contort accordingly. If you're hiding parts of yourself, your body will attempt to shrink. When you allow those hidden parts to come out and play, your body will be open because it has nothing to fear. You will feel confident about who you are, wherever you go.

Observe when you hold back from sharing different parts of yourself. For example, let's say you don't want to show the part of you that gets angry to your partner. So you pretend that everything is OK (when it's not) and build up resentment. Even-tually, you walk away from the relationship or let it slowly die. Instead, next time that you notice you're holding back from ex-pressing your anger, pause and then ask this simple question out loud: "Which part of me am I hiding right now?" Respond truthfully: "I'm hiding the part of me that is angry." Become cu-rious and ask, "What does the part of you that is angry want to say out loud?" Pause. Allow your anger to surface and speak through you: "I feel betrayed, and I'm angry that I keep getting hurt like this."

As you continue to converse with yourself out loud, simply remain open to what your hidden part has to say; allow it to ex-press its needs. Using the example of speaking to the part of you that hides your anger, maybe it says back to you, "All I want is for someone to hear how I feel. I have been carrying this anger inside me, and I just need to let it out, but I don't know how." You're deepening intimacy with yourself, and it might feel like you're opening a Pandora's box of all your dark secrets. Saying it out loud will shine a light on those parts of yourself that you've been judging and hiding; they will be set free when spoken to with curiosity and openness. The more you seek to understand the parts of yourself that you've hidden, the more at home you will feel in your body. You won't need to hide anymore, because you've sought to understand rather than judge.

Speaking to yourself in a playful tone of voice is essential to saying it out loud, especially as you're cultivating understanding and acceptance of your flaws. Think about it this way. Have you ever walked into a room and almost instantly felt like you didn't belong there? Every fiber of your being was uneasy because you didn't feel like you fit in. You left after less than ten minutes (or didn't even make it through the front door). Now, imagine that you've just walked into the same room and a friend comes up to you and cheerfully says, "Hi! I haven't seen you in so long! You look fabulous! How are you?" Would you end up staying? Most likely yes, because you feel welcomed and wanted. This is why using a playful tone of voice will help rebuild trust with the parts of yourself that you've exiled. Every part of you needs to feel welcomed and wanted by YOU in order for you to show up as your most confident and authentic self.

Channel Your Hidden Parts

One of the greatest gifts you can give yourself is permission to channel and transform the energy that you've been using to hide your parts into something constructive, expressive, and creative. For example, many experiences in my life hardened my heart. I used to spend a lot of energy protecting my heart from ever getting hurt again. I put on a facade of "nothing ever bothers me." When I stopped pretending as if nothing ever bothered me and said out loud how I was actually feeling, which was hurt and lonely, that part of me felt so much lighter, and I was able to channel that energy into my creative passions, like acting, voice-over work, and writing. It was through expressing myself in these creative and playful ways that I was able to heal so many of the parts of me that wanted to come alive. Acknowledging and allowing those parts of you to be expressed frees you up to create something new in your life.

For you to feel fully integrated, each and every single part of you needs to be expressed and playfully channeled in a way that expands these parts of you, not diminishes the fullness of your expression. Maybe you used to love theater and dramatic arts, but as you got older you hid that theatrical part of you, and now you've become somewhat of a gossip and drama queen. You know that you have this part of you that loves to gossip, but you don't know how to change it. Ask yourself, "What does this part of me actually crave?" When you take the time to get curious about yourself, you'll realize that the behavior you're exhibiting is nothing more than misdirected energy. Maybe you've been wanting to take a dance class. But there's a part of you that is terrified of looking stupid in front of anyone else. So you hold back from taking the dance class. You're hiding not only the part of you that really wants to dance but also the part of you that fears messing up in front of people. In this instance, instead of channeling this part of you creatively, you're continuing to per-petuate the narrative that "this part of me is bad and needs to be hidden."

For many of us, trying new things, such as group activities, brings up a *lot* of fear. The solution isn't to isolate, to never go out and socialize. The solution is to understand the level of support your hidden parts need so that they can be playfully channeled. Playfully channeling your hidden parts can happen through competitive sports, dancing, acting, kickboxing, screaming at the top of your lungs, performing comedy, writing, running in the park, jumping into a pool, striking up a conversation with strangers — really anything that gets you out of your head and into your free-spirited, childlike nature.

Keep Cool with Your Inner Critic

OK, so let's say you've talked yourself through your fears and are now signed up for your very first adult dance class (*woo-hoo!*) or your choice of new experience. As you're getting ready to head out the door, you hear a voice inside you that says, "Why are you even doing this? What's the point? Why are you wasting your money on a dance class? You're an adult. Act like one." *Oof.* That's the cynical voice inside that manages to suck the fun out of anything that may be slightly out of your normal routine. It's the voice that keeps us from trying new things, playing like kids, and exploring different parts of us. Instead of giving up before you even start, you can ask yourself, "What's the best thing that can come out of taking a dance class?" Speak to the part of you that is nervous. In those moments, ask yourself out loud, "What do I need in order to have fun again?" or "What part of me is afraid to come out and play?" You're talking to yourself in a way that is moving you toward what you want, rather than staying stuck in fear.

Practice using this gentler approach as you dialogue with your inner cynic. If you've been harsh with yourself and it hasn't worked up until this point, maybe it's time to play with a different style of communication. In those moments of fear, playfully converse with yourself as you would with a friend or a young child, out loud. "It sounds like you're nervous about taking this class. Talk to me. What's going on?" Can you feel the cool, light-hearted nature of that question? Don't shut down on yourself. When your inner cynic creeps in, rather than shutting it up or letting it have complete control over you, pause and confidently say it out loud.

Verbalize the internal conversation of the part of you that is nervous to try new things, be seen, and potentially feel embarrassed. But to allow that part of you to open, you will need to *befriend the voice of your cynic*, which is just another part of you that is overprotective and terrified of being humiliated. Even your inner cynic is worthy of your kindness, because it is just another part of you. And until you learn how to speak to that part of you, anytime you want to try new things or start expressing more or being vulnerable, that voice will pop up. Do not for another second allow the often-unhelpful voices in your head to continue to rule your life. It's time to replace them with a fresh voice that is eager to live and be creatively expressed.

Lead with Your Hidden Parts

Imagine how free you would feel in any situation if you stopped trying to manage parts of yourself and, instead, allowed those parts to shine brightly. For example, say you have a comedic side that you rarely show to others. At work, you've been called "uptight" and "high-strung" by your colleagues. The point here is not to focus on what your colleagues said but to use it as information to learn more about yourself. Contemplate for a moment how work would feel if you allowed more of your comedic side to come out, rather than keeping it hidden. Or maybe you are a very deep feeler, but you hide that part of yourself in your professional life because you want people to take you seriously. Consider here that your sensitivity, your ability to feel deeply, is what will enable you to build solid foundations for your relationships. Somewhere along the way, you believed that it was safer to hide those parts of yourself than to lead with them. Start leading with the parts that you have left behind. What you've been presenting to the world is your inauthentic self. It's the self that you've refined through the years to get by, keep the peace, and keep people in your life, no matter how one-sided or toxic the relationships have become. It's exhausting to expend so much energy on hiding and lying to the world about who you *really* are. I'd rather you take the time to be real with yourself than fight the truth of who you are.

As you begin to speak with your hidden parts, you'll start to think more clearly and have so much energy that you'll feel like you want to burst. That's because those parts you've hidden are nothing more than stuck energy in your body waiting to be expressed. It's as if they're saying to you, "Hey, remember me? Can I come out now?" You have the power to transform your life when you create the stage for all your parts to be seen, heard, and expressed.

The supportive, encouraging, and compassionate side that you show to the people in your life can be accessed *at anytime* by prompting yourself with a question out loud and allowing whatever comes up to express itself. Essentially, you're giving a voice to every single part of you, just as you would with a friend. You don't judge your friends if they share a vulnerable side of themselves, do you? The way that you already know how to show understanding and compassion to others is exactly what you're being invited to do with yourself. In doing so, you'll get to bring your fully integrated self into every situation. You have the ability to heal all the parts of yourself, using the power of your voice coupled with your willingness to understand yourself on a deep level.

The healthiest relationships take time, empathy, and a willingness to learn. Remember, this isn't about being perfect. It's about talking to yourself in a way that opens the door for an authentic response within you. The way you do that is by getting curious with yourself as you would with a small child who is afraid of monsters under their bed. Find your unique voice for speaking to the hidden parts of you, infusing it with a spirited and light tone. The vibe for the exercises is intended to be playful. How much fun can you have with your hidden parts? Be willing to play with your voice, inflection, tone, and volume as you go through these exercises. Play to learn, grow, have fun, and seek self-understanding.

Hopefully by now you are feeling a lot more love for yourself! With compassion and joy, you are now tending to the parts of you that you hid out of shame or fear and are integrating them into your healthy whole. Going forward in our work, it is time to start *choosing yourself* — falling truly in love with yourself and having the confidence and courage to build the life of your dreams.

SAY IT OUT LOUD EXERCISE

Prompt: Notice the types of situations and interactions where you hide parts of yourself. Observe the situations when you feel constricted or closed off and those when you feel open. Pay attention to when you feel most like yourself versus when you feel like you have something to shield.

Practice: Ask yourself out loud, "Which part of me am I hiding right now?" or "What parts of myself do I not want other people to see?" Pause and be patient with the parts of you that don't quite trust it's safe to come out and play.

Here's an example of how that dialogue might go.

"Which part of me am I hiding right now?"

"I am hiding the part of me that doesn't ever want anyone to know that I feel inadequate."

"How does feeling inadequate show up in my life?"

"Well, I often find myself doubting my every move. I worry that I won't make good decisions. And I'm always in fear that people will get bored or tired of me and eventually leave."

"What do I do to hide my inadequacies?"

"I act like everything is fine, I feel silly asking for help because that makes me feel stupid, and I overcompensate to prove that I am good enough."

"If I wasn't trying to hide the part of me that feels inadequate, how would I be showing up differently?"

"*I would walk into the room with confidence. I wouldn't hesitate to ask for help if I needed it.*"

"And? What else?"

"*I would trust my intuition. Life would feel so much more fun and playful.*"

"Keep going…"

"*I wouldn't feel the need to prove my worth, because I know that I bring value to the table. I wouldn't be in a constant state of proving all the time. I would relax and trust that who I am is more than enough. Like, I wouldn't have to try so hard to be accepted.*"

"What does the part of you that feels inadequate need from me?" (This is where you get to practice loving compassion toward yourself.)

"*The part of me that feels inadequate needs me to slow down and celebrate all the things I've created up until this point. I need to start acknowledging myself, rather than thinking there is something wrong with me.*"

"What's something fun we could do together to celebrate?"

"*Hmm, a Sunday morning walk with coffee sounds amazing.*"

This is an actual conversation I had with myself. Replace "Sunday morning walk with coffee" with anything playful and fun that will help you build the relationship with the part of yourself that is hidden. Once you hear from yourself what you need, follow through and give that to yourself within the week! Do not wait! Self-trust strengthens every time you follow through with yourself. This is why you say it out loud. Because once you hear it, you can't unhear it; you can't keep lying to yourself.

Promise: Promise that you'll try to be more playful and curious with yourself. Commit to following through with whatever you express out loud. You're building trust with a part of you that needs to feel safe to come out and express itself.

SAY IT OUT LOUD AFFIRMATIONS

I can be powerful and ask for help at the same time.
I don't have to be perfect to be lovable.
Every time I acknowledge my inner child, a part of me heals.
Not everyone has to like me or accept me. I just have to like and accept me.

Chapter 10

CHOOSE YOURSELF OUT LOUD

Answer this out loud:
Do you feel selfish when you do things just for you?

In ninth grade, my father moved me from public to private school. I was never part of the cool girls' club back in my other school, so I was eager to make new friends. I decided that I would become the funny, likable, public school transplant Indian girl and leave behind the parts of me that were often made fun of by my old classmates. I accomplished this by figuring out exactly who I needed to be in order to fit in with whatever clique I was trying to be a part of.

I went from being the outsider to finally feeling like I fit in. I was being invited to sleepovers, parties, and other social gatherings that were previously not even on my radar. For once, my tired teenage self felt like she belonged. But it came with a price. In order to feel like I belonged, I thought I had to abandon who I was. I have so much compassion for the teenage Vasavi who thought that she was "too Indian" or "different" and felt like she had to choose between being liked or being herself. Needless to say, I was confused. At school I was just hoping to be liked. At home, I didn't know how to blend my Indian side with my more Western side. Every time I wanted to go hang out with my friends, my father would say to me, "Your family comes first. You're being selfish for not taking us into account. We don't feel comfortable with you sleeping at your friend's house. Stop being selfish." As a teenager who was trying to find some sense of identity and belonging, my intention was never to be selfish or disregard my family. All I wanted was to feel accepted at school, have friends, and be invited to the occasional sleepover. As in most immigrant families, "Don't question your elders ever" was our motto. But I couldn't have disagreed more. At a young age, I often asked myself, "Am I bad for wanting to do what I want to do?" And while I now know that my father, influenced by his cultural upbringing, was being protective of me, his words would set off a series of events in my life that stemmed from the belief that I was selfish for choosing to do what made me happy.

Even if you have never been called selfish, you may have witnessed your mother prioritizing everyone else's needs over her own, only to end up frazzled, irritable, and tired. And when you saw her tired, you felt like it was your responsibility to take care of her. Or maybe you feel guilty because you've never really had to struggle in your life, so when you desire more in your career, finances, relationships, or creative pursuits, you tell yourself, "I should just be happy with what I have." Or you feel pulled in so many directions that even the idea of allotting time and space just for yourself feels absurd, even wrong at times. Whatever your situation is, the point that I want to drive home in this chapter is that sacrificing your own mental and emotional health for the sake of others will cost you the time and energy required to courageously choose what is best for *you*.

When I set out to write this book, I wanted to convey a very clear message: your voice, and how you use it to talk to yourself, has the power to change your life. In each and every moment that you exist, you have the power to choose your thoughts, how you respond to those thoughts, and how you live your life. If you've ever felt like choosing yourself is selfish, my hope is that by the end of this chapter, you will realize that choosing to honor the truth of who you are sets the standard, tone, and flow for your life.

Life can get busy with family, social obligations, our careers, and everything that we are experiencing as a collective. It can often feel like we have zero control over what is occurring. The one thing we do have control over is how we choose to respond. The best way I have found to take back our power to choose is by setting up meaningful practices, from how we begin our morning to how we end the day. Additionally, having hobbies for pure enjoyment gives us a chance to choose ourselves, because even when things get tough, we can always count on our hobbies to bring us a sense of internal peace. In this chapter, you will learn how to speak to the part of you that prioritizes everyone and everything else before you. I will be placing an emphasis on choosing how you start and end your day, and the hobbies that you have, as ways to start putting your happiness first.

Do you believe that it is selfish to choose yourself?

According to Merriam-Webster, *selfish* means "concerned excessively or exclusively with oneself: seeking or concentrating on one's own advantage, pleasure, or well-being without regard for others."

What if "without regard for others" was actually a *good* thing? What if you made choices with the utmost regard for *you* rather than taking everyone else into account? Most of us consider the impact of our decisions on others without taking into consideration how they'll affect our own well-being. And while being selfless is often celebrated in our society, if you want to maximize the positive results for everyone, including you, you need to psychologically distance yourself from your decision and look at the potential big-picture impact. The best way to do this is to speak your choices out loud. When you step back and consider the big picture out loud, you can evaluate the possible consequences and decide how to best allocate your time, energy, and attention.

Choosing to do what is best for you will initially feel uncomfortable. Notice the discomfort in your body when you feel torn between what you know you need to be working on and your impulse to allow yourself to get distracted. When you feel this in your body, ask yourself out loud, "What choice would be for my highest good right now?" Asking this question will keep you honest with yourself, because when you say it out loud, it is much harder to deny that choosing yourself will always be the best decision for you.

If you don't choose yourself, who will?

The time and energy you choose to give to *other* people, solve *their* problems, listen to *their* ideas, and provide encouragement for *their* dreams keep you from working on your own dreams. I'm not saying never to lend an ear to a friend in need. I'm drawing your attention to the idea that it's easier to give our time, energy, and attention to others, because we are more emotionally detached from the success of their outcomes than we are to the possibility of failing at our own goals. Maybe there are areas of your life where you are already prioritizing yourself first, but when it comes to your dreams of starting a business or completing the creative project that you've been putting off, you struggle with making yourself the number one priority.

The reason so many of us are willing to be available to others is so that we don't have to tend to our own life. The irony is, we feel accomplished and good for lending a hand to others but feel guilty for focusing on creating our own life. Not choosing ourselves allows us to stay safe, small, hidden, and free from judgment if our plans don't work out. It allows us to avoid potential humiliation and any questioning from others, like, "Who do you think you are to do/say that?"

Even when you're feeling emotionally, energetically, and/or mentally drained from being available to everyone else, you can still deny that there is any payoff, because you're being a "good person" just trying to help others — you're operating from the narrative that says you should sacrifice yourself for others, even at the expense of your own well-being. If you're exhausted from being available to others, you'll have a plethora of excuses and distractions that keep you from being accountable in your own life.

Everything we do has a payoff. Every story we have about ourselves, others, and situations keeps that energy alive in our life. Now, why would any logical person continue to repeat a behavior that clearly isn't serving them? As long as we keep focusing our energy on the people in our lives and how they're the "problem," we never really have to tend to ourselves. Every time you notice yourself complaining, gossiping, or talking about your ideas rather than working on them, take a pause, then ask yourself out loud, "Is this the best use of my time and energy?" You will notice that it clearly is not the best use of your time and energy, and even more so, that the spaciousness to create what you want in your life expands as you live according to your priorities.

Surrender to Your Higher Self

Internal conflict keeps us from choosing ourselves. When you're conflicted, the back-and-forth voices in your head about what you should and shouldn't do can drown out the voice of your Higher Self, which will guide you to do what is best for you. For my client Dana, her conflict was that she wanted to be alone for the holidays but was experiencing deeply embedded guilt and shame for making a decision that was healthy for her.

"Vasavi," she told me, "I feel so emotionally heavy. I don't want to be around my family for Christmas. I don't want to deal with their criticism and judgment. But I feel bad not going because, you know, we're this big Italian family, and Christmas is our thing." Dana had recently divorced her husband, was transitioning in her career, and was moving through a barrage of emotions. Her family dynamics were complicated, and every part of Dana was pleading for her to just stay put in her own home instead of seeing her family.

"Dana, what would your Higher Self choose for you?" I asked.

She paused for a moment and then said, "My Higher Self would choose space and time to be with myself." Dana was clear on what she needed.

"Now that you know the choice you want to make, what's next?"

She responded, "I need to be honest with my family and let them know I am spending the holidays with myself." Even though she was uncomfortable letting her family down, Dana chose herself in that moment. She decided to spend the holidays in solitude to process her grief without having her family constantly breathing down her neck. Dana acknowledged out loud the fear and trepidation she was experiencing simply at the thought of being with her family for the holidays. She then admitted the internal conflict that was keeping her stuck: "This is what I 'should' do" versus "But this is what I want to do."

There is no easy way to choose yourself. We've been groomed from day one of our existence to emotionally cater to the needs of others at the cost of our own desires. We betray and abandon ourselves to make everyone around us feel comfortable, even though internally we're engaging in emotional and spiritual warfare against ourselves. And therein lies the duality within us. It's in those moments of feeling internally conflicted that we can speak out loud to prompt those parts of us that feel scared, guilty, and insecure and hear what each part has to say. Asking yourself out loud, "What is best for *me*?" will set the foundation for a truthful dialogue with your Higher Self. You might feel uncomfortable answering that question because you are not in the habit of choosing yourself first. When you notice this discomfort, simply say out loud, "I'm noticing that in this moment, I am experiencing discomfort expressing what is best for me." Pause, acknowledge how that feels in your body, get curious, and address yourself by name: "[Insert your name], if you were completely free from worry about how choosing yourself might impact others, what would you choose?" Take a deep breath and relax. This is where you practice surrendering to your Higher Self. All you're doing is allowing yourself to receive guidance from a part of you that knows your truth and what you need most for your own evolution. It is the wisest part of you, the part that chooses from a place of utmost love and care for your well-being.

This type of question is eye-opening for two reasons. First, by saying, "If you were completely free from worrying about how choosing yourself might impact others," you are eliminating one of the biggest concerns, which is the undeniable fear of choosing yourself over others. Second, when you address yourself by name, it takes you out of your egocentric view and helps to regulate your emotions.

Stop identifying as the "I" that is struggling with the internal conflict of making a choice that is best for you, and you will begin to see clearly and take a more objective approach to your choices. Consciously choosing to be patient and to speak to yourself with understanding will calm your nervous system. Ask yourself questions with kindness and curiosity, just as you would with a friend, mentee, client, or loved one who came to you with the same dilemma. Feel free to take on the voice of an encouraging coach and say to yourself out loud, "[Insert your name], you got this. It takes courage to choose yourself. Focus on you." Experiment with what works for you and, most importantly, have fun with how you speak to yourself.

> **Become unavailable for things that don't fit where you're going.**

When you start to prioritize your projects and commitments, inevitably you will come across distractions in many different forms. Don't get sidetracked. Distractions are an opportunity for us to become even more rooted and stay true to ourselves. When you find yourself in situations and conversations that no longer fit where you're going, say this out loud: "I am no longer available for this."

Choosing you is a habit that can be cultivated. And yes, people may think you're selfish. But, honestly, it doesn't even matter. What matters is that you're being true to yourself, and if some people label that as selfish, so be it. When you start to put yourself at the top of your priority list, you'll notice how much of your energy has been spent on things that don't light you up. Conversations that used to eat away at your time and energy suddenly feel intolerably draining, so you become more intentional with your time and energy. Requests that you used to say yes to are now opportunities for you to discern between distractions and values-based decisions.

Choose Yourself in the Morning

When I got out of rehab in 2019, I had nowhere to go but forward. I had zero clients; my mom was paying for everything; and my relationship with my ex-fiancé was basically over. I sat in front of my laptop and searched, "How do I love myself?" I kept seeing articles on having routines and rituals. I was super triggered because I knew that self-love practices were completely missing from my life. I craved safety and stability yet had no idea where to begin. I was resistant to building my foundation.

From practicing yoga and meditation to creating personal and professional goals, pulling tarot cards, and listening to podcasts, all the information pertaining to this one question "How do I love myself?" overwhelmed me. I got up, walked into my kitchen, stood at the counter, and asked myself out loud, "What does loving Vasavi look like every single day?" Do you want to know the answer that came? The very first thing I made a habit of doing in the morning was drinking my Morning Elixir.

Vasavi's Morning Elixir

Ingredients

    32 ounces filtered water
    ¼ teaspoon pink Himalayan salt
    Juice of 1 lemon

Mix ingredients in a mason jar. Enjoy!

First act of self-love: check!

I did that for ninety days straight, and it's still to this day an integral part of my self-love plan. The first step will often be the simplest. Do not let that deter you from starting. If you notice yourself thinking, "This is too easy," then respond out loud, "Let it be easy then." Our minds tend to complicate things that require only a simple step to move us toward loving ourselves.

How you start and end your day sets the tone for everything that happens in between. Tuning in to the ebb and flow of your energetic rhythm will help you create your most supportive morning routine. And know that as the seasons change, you will find yourself craving a new morning experience. Don't hold yourself to a fixed idea that there's a "right" and "wrong" way to start your morning. In designing your morning routine, you can choose what works for you and change it up when your needs change. As you start to get more connected to your emotional and physical body, calming your nervous system by speaking to yourself in a loving and soothing way, ask yourself out loud, "How do we want our mornings to feel?" If you hear any thoughts such as, "I don't have time to do this!" or "But what about the kids?" or "I'm not a morning person," you get to *choose* how you respond to those thoughts.

Choosing how you respond might sound like you acknowledging out loud: "I know that this is all very new for you, but it's going to be healthy for us to start our mornings this way." Or it might sound like: "Stop with the excuses. Let's figure out how we want to start our mornings." Pick whichever approach motivates you to move forward. If a no-nonsense, direct voice works for you, then use that! If a harsh tone doesn't work for you, then don't use it. You're at the point where you're committed to making decisions, creating habits, and developing hobbies. The only thing getting in the way is what you're telling yourself about what's possible. Refrain from putting an immense amount of pressure on your routine to be "perfect." Experiment to find what works for you. Test it out. Evaluate it to see what's working, and feel free to change your mind.

Picture This

Your alarm goes off. You slowly raise your arms overhead and stretch your legs out long in front of you. You blink your eyes a few times to adjust to the sunlight streaming in. On the nightstand next to you is a carafe of water waiting to quench your thirst and kickstart your digestive system. You gently sit upright and spend a few minutes practicing deep breathing to connect with yourself, then you say out loud, "I am grateful to be alive. Today is a beautiful day." You brush your teeth, wash your face, put on walking shoes, and head out the door to move your body for a few minutes with a brisk walk, using the sun to energize you before you head back home to get ready for the day.

Your routine is just another area of your life where you get to practice choosing yourself before giving to others. You may feel like you don't have time to perform a morning routine because you have a job to get to and kids who need to be dropped off at school. Be mindful of any thoughts that sound like:

- "I don't want to get up earlier."
- "What's the point of all of this routine stuff?"
- "Is this yet another thing I have to do? I am so tired."
- "I don't even know where to begin."

These thoughts are nothing more than the voice of resistance. (Revisit chapter 7 for a refresher on how to respond to the voice of resistance out loud.)

You Get to Set the Tone for the Day

If you find yourself spending way too much time overthinking and perfecting your morning routine, try this. Start following humans on social media who inspire you. Social media can serve as an excellent resource on your self-love journey. Borrow inspiration from bloggers and content creators and ask yourself out loud, "How do I want to feel in the morning?" From there ask yourself, "What would a beautiful morning routine look like for me?" You can choose which accounts you follow. Notice what draws you to some people. Is it because they have certain qualities that you wish to embody? Or do you love how much attention to detail they place on creating a beautiful space where they meditate? Or maybe you are inspired by their healthy eating and fitness practices. Pay close attention to the sparks that you feel inside. If a particular activity or morning practice ignites the spark inside you, follow it!

Hobbies are healthy and an integral act of self-love.

As adults we forget that often it's the simplest joys in life that bring us the most pleasure. Reconnecting with the childlike essence inside you is key to prioritizing your needs. Your joy needs no explanation or reason. It is simply yours to experience. Incorporating hobbies into your life that bring you pure joy is the epitome of choosing yourself, because you're doing something just for *you*. And that is why you need them. You need things in your life that are just for you and no one else.

Below is a mini-written exercise that you can recreate on your own. Each heading is a question meant for you to ask out loud. For example, ask yourself out loud, "What is something fun I've been wanting to do?" Let your mind just wander and imagine! If you know off the top of your head that you've been wanting to go on a solo vacation, then write that down. Maybe you've been wanting to take up a new sport, like tennis! The point here is to allow yourself to have fun because that's the point of hobbies. Notice when you get into the trap of conjuring a logical reason for wanting something. Allow yourself simply to desire, imagine, and dream. Then, follow through with bringing your desires to life. Start with the very best next simple step.

Even the act of sitting down and investing the time and energy to fill out the chart can bring up thoughts such as, "Is this really going to make a difference in my life?" or "This seems too simple." By now, I think it's fair to say you're seeing that thoughts run in the background of your mind as you forge the path to courageously pursuing your dreams. You can choose to entertain these thoughts and ask out loud, "What's going on?" to start a dialogue with yourself. Perhaps one part of you responds, "What's the point of all of this? Why are you making me do this?" This is your voice of resistance (see chapter 7), and you can continue to converse to get to the root of the resistance, or you can use a firmer approach and say, "Stop with the negative attitude and let's focus."

There will be times when you need a gentle approach, and there will be times when you need to coach yourself through major resistance. Paying attention to how you feel in your body, plus being clear on your priorities and commitments, helps you to move through resistance quickly. Honor how you feel and keep moving forward. In life, you are going to come across plenty of things you do not want to do because they are hard work, are time-consuming, and require your focus. But in those moments, you get to *choose* on the basis of the future that you are creating for yourself. You always have the power to choose what you focus on.

From there, ask yourself out loud, "When am I going to do this?" This is your "by when date." Once you pick a date (do not skip this step!), put it down in your calendar in your phone or write it down in your planner. This is a very important step because no date means no plan. Mark a date on your calendar so it becomes real. Then ask yourself, "What are my current beliefs?" You may not have any sort of current beliefs that are holding you back, so skip this step if no feelings of guilt or hesitation show up. However, if you do have limiting beliefs, such as that you are selfish for choosing yourself, then you can say out loud whatever you are experiencing in the moment. Next, shift your perspective by asking yourself out loud, "What is another way of looking at this?" Once again, you have an opportunity to *choose* your thoughts and how you respond to them. Tap into the wise, sage-like part of you and respond, "Honoring my desires is my birthright" or "It's about time I take a vacation."

In the beginning, choosing yourself might feel uncomfortable. In those moments, tune in to what your body is feeling and how your mind is responding. Notice how you feel and observe your thoughts. If what you're telling yourself isn't moving you forward, *choose* to shift how you're thinking by saying the thought out loud, then asking yourself an expansive question — one that will help shift and open your perspective to guide you closer to what you want. Finally, ask yourself, "What is the first simple step I will take?" The action that you need to take will most likely be the simplest step. Do not overcomplicate it.

MINI–WRITTEN EXERCISE: PERSPECTIVE SHIFT

In this exercise, you will map your desires on paper. Answer these questions, following the examples provided below.

1. **Hobby:** What's something fun I've been wanting to do?
2. **Timing:** By what date am I going to do this?
3. **Current Belief(s):** What are my existing limiting beliefs about doing this?
4. **Perspective Shift:** What is another way of looking at this?
5. **Simple Step:** What is the first simple step I will take?

Example 1

1. **Hobby:** Solo traveling to different countries.
2. **Timing:** I will take my first trip by [insert specific date].
3. **Current Belief(s):** (A) I'm selfish for leaving my kids behind. (B) It's a waste of money.
4. **Perspective Shift:** Honoring my desires is my birthright.
5. **Simple Step:** Pick a place I've been wanting to visit.

Example 2

1. **Hobby:** Start a book club with my friends.
2. **Timing:** Feb 1.
3. **Current Belief(s):** (A) No one will come. (B) I don't have time to start a book club let alone read a book.
4. **Perspective Shift:** (A) There are people in my life who would really love to get together and be a part of this. (B) I've been saying I want to read and socialize more, so this is a great way to do both!
5. **Simple Step:** Make a list of people to invite.

Notice under "Perspective Shift" there is no rationalization or justification. It doesn't say, "The more I tend to my desires, the more I'm able to give others." While choosing yourself will indeed allow you to have more capacity for others, that's not the reason why you need to be selfish. You need to be selfish because you are your most valuable asset. And without you, your life is nonexistent. It's more than OK to choose yourself simply because you said so. A vacation doesn't need to be justified by tying it to some bigger purpose. You're worthy of a solo vacation (or whatever exemplifies you choosing yourself) because that's what you want and you're in charge of your life.

Hobbies give you an opportunity to reconnect with the parts of you that crave fun, pleasure, and freedom. You are the single greatest asset into which you could ever invest your time, money, and energy. Use your hobbies as an outlet for your creativity to move through. Train yourself to be curious and be willing to try new things, simply because it sparks something inside you. Challenge the voices in your head that disconnect you from yourself. You do not need to justify why you want what you want. You just need to be extremely honest with yourself about what you want, and if applicable, why you can't have it. Invest in your mind, body, spirit, and creativity. You are worth investing in.

It's not going to be easy to put your desires first. In good conscience I can't sit here and tell you that the people around you will accept this new version of you — someone who is reprioritizing, creating clear boundaries, and choosing themselves first. You might receive pushback and hear things like, "Wow, you've really changed," as if staying the same should be worn like a badge of honor. Instead of allowing those comments to make you doubt your decisions to put yourself first, celebrate the person you're becoming and say out loud, "Yup! And I feel great!" Celebrate your dedication and commitment to healing your soul. Surround yourself with people who are on a similar path of healing, reprogramming belief systems, and courageously pursuing their dreams.

The Say It Out Loud exercise at the end of this chapter should be done in a quiet and calm environment. Practice this exercise before you're about to have a difficult conversation, speak up for yourself, say no, walk away from a toxic relationship, or set boundaries — basically, any situation where you have historically swept aside your needs, assumed the responsibility for managing other people's emotions, and betrayed yourself. How you talk to yourself determines how you feel about yourself. How you feel determines the actions you take (or do not take). And at the end of the day, you still have the power to choose what is best for you. Start small and build your self-worth and self-love day by day, choice by choice.

In the next chapter we will apply these concepts to real-world, specific situations. Beyond simply understanding how to choose ourselves, we must learn to engage with life in a manner that reflects our newfound confidence and self-love. We will take a look at some ways that we can decide to pursue our authentic desires in our lives.

SAY IT OUT LOUD EXERCISE

Prompt: Notice any situation where you have deemed it wrong to choose yourself first or speak up for your needs. For example:

- Declining a social invitation because you would rather spend time with yourself.
- Accepting a social invitation that would open the door to new connections and relationships.
- Releasing the responsibility to take on a colleague's workload.
- Surrendering the need to manage other people's emotions.
- Creating boundaries in your personal and professional life.
- Receiving compliments, gifts, and offers to help you.
- No longer being available for one-sided relationships.
- Asking for exactly what you want at a restaurant (or at work or in relationships).

Practice: When presented with a choice where you would typically consider others before putting yourself first:

1. Ask yourself out loud, "What do I want in this situation?"

2. As your thoughts come to the surface, fully hear each thought, give it a voice, and say it out loud. Based on my personal experience and conversations with clients, here are some of the thoughts that typically come up when asking this question out loud:

   - "But what about…?"
   - "I can't do that…"
   - "Where would I begin?"
   - "I don't deserve…"

3. This is where you get to practice self-distancing. Objectively hear your concerns out, just as you would with a friend. Talk with yourself. Try on different viewpoints and scenarios.

4. Ask yourself or say out loud any of the following phrases while you're dialoguing with yourself. It's OK to take a moment to ground yourself before responding.

   - What do I want more than anything in the world?
   - What is the best-case scenario if I choose myself?
   - What would I do today if I chose myself?
   - "It is safe for me to choose myself."
   - "I am practicing honoring my needs."
   - "I'm choosing myself, and it feels really good."
   - "I'm proud of myself for being courageous and choosing myself."

Promise: Promise to choose you. Every single time. Not just occasionally or when you feel like you're worthy of your own kindness. All the time. There are going to be days when you slip back into patterns of self-criticism and judgment. You're not falling behind or failing if you have a few days when you aren't so kind to yourself. Even in those moments, notice how you're treating yourself and keep choosing kindness. Forgive yourself. Be gentle with yourself.

SAY IT OUT LOUD AFFIRMATIONS

Choosing myself is an act of self-love.
Every time I speak my truth and choose to prioritize my well-being, the relationship with myself becomes stronger.
I follow my heart, not the expectations of others.

Chapter 11

DESIRE AND DECIDE OUT LOUD

Answer this out loud:
Do you feel guilty expressing your true desires?

Remember that heart-wrenching scene in the movie *The Notebook*? If you haven't seen it, please watch it (after you finish reading this book, of course). And if you have seen it, then you probably know what scene I'm referring to. Noah asks Allie, "What do you want?" She stares back at him, flustered because she can't give him a clear answer. Noah continues to ask her, "What do you want?!" Everyone watching the movie knows that Allie deep down wants to be with Noah. But she's scared. Her parents disapprove of him. She's afraid of losing the comfort of her wealth. The safety and security of what she's familiar with are clearly driving her to deny herself what she really wants.

It's painfully familiar and frustrating to watch, because so many of us have been in some version of that scene. We're asked what we want, and we freeze. Or our mind is flooded with a plethora of options, based on what other people will think or whether what we want is valid. Or maybe the idea of even being asked what you want — much less asking yourself out loud, "What do I want?" — is mind-boggling because you don't remember the last time you took your desires into consideration.

Do you relate to Allie? When asked, "What do you want?" do you freeze? Do you start thinking about the opinions of your family, friends, and colleagues? Does your mind immediately tell you that you can't have what you want? Do you run through all the possible what-if scenarios? If you answered yes to any of these questions, I want you to breathe. You are not alone in your thinking. Many of us have made decisions that didn't align with our truest desires. Instead, they were based on our level of self-worth and self-esteem. The truth is, it's easy to blame other people for why our lives look a certain way, but if you delve deeper inside, you'll find that every decision you have made up until this point was determined by what you believed you were worthy of. The intention of this chapter is to help you align your decisions with your desires. You will learn how to connect with your desires and how to get clear on your decisions, out loud. It is your birthright to desire and make decisions that are congruent with the person you are becoming.

> Hesitation to say it out loud is
> an opportunity to ask for guidance.

Anytime you feel a deep desire to create something that speaks to you, whether it be art, love, or taking your career to the next level, you might find yourself hesitating. In fact, as quickly as you felt your spark, you will be met with hesitation. This hesitation that we experience shows up in two ways: the hesitation to speak our desires out loud and the hesitation to take the next step.

Let's look at both.

Hesitation #1: Speaking Our Desires Out Loud

My first-ever mentor and coach, Lisa Nichols, once invited me to share my desires out loud in front of a group of fifteen female entrepreneurs. I remember feeling so small and nervous. I was terrified to speak my story out loud. Embarrassed by my bipolar disorder diagnosis, I hesitated to reveal my deepest desires of helping as many people as possible. I thought my dreams were too big or that people would say, "Who does she think she is?" Eventually I mustered my courage and said, "I want to help as many people as possible through my speaking and writing!"

The irony is that I wanted to be able to help as many people as possible with their confidence and self-expression, yet here I was lacking confidence in my own self-expression. Saying my desires out loud made them *real*. Funny how that works, right? The very thing we desire the most requires us to examine what scares us the most. In stating out loud my desire to help other people step into the fullest expression of themselves, I had to examine my own fear of full self-expression and what that meant for me.

We hesitate to say what we desire out loud for many reasons. First, we are afraid that once we say it, we're responsible for following through. On a deeper level, it is much more about our inability to see ourselves as powerful creators of our lives; we doubt our capacity and ability to bring our desires to life. Second, we are hesitant to speak our desires out loud because we have become accustomed to ignoring them. Start observing when, where, and with whom you hold back from expressing your desires out loud. Acknowledging that might sound like, "I'm noticing that I am hesitant in speaking my desires out loud." The act of saying this out loud allows you to empty your mind and reconnect with your body.

Hesitation #2: Taking the Next Step

If you feel hesitant to take action toward your desires, do not interpret that as going in the wrong direction; do not give up before you even start. Notice when you hesitate, and rather than giving up on your desires, ask yourself out loud, "What is this hesitation about?" Maybe you don't feel equipped with certain skills, or maybe you need support in figuring out a strategy, or maybe you would benefit from further clarification on next steps. Respond truthfully out loud, "I am feeling hesitant because [insert your hesitation]." By having this conversation out loud, you're not allowing your hesitation to stop you. Instead, you're getting curious about why you're hesitating and working with yourself to understand what you would need to no longer feel hesitant. This is where you begin to trust and rely on your ability to find support and solutions to help you bring your desires to life.

What you desire desires you right back.

Unbeknownst to most people, I absolutely love binge-watching dance videos and Oscar and Grammy Award acceptance speeches. I get lost in the words of the performer thanking everyone who has helped them reach this point of recognition and honor. I am mesmerized by how one human being can become a character and embody the essence of the role they're playing. It's pure play in motion.

One night, I was watching Matthew McConaughey accept his Best Actor Oscar for *Dallas Buyers Club*. In his speech he talked about the three things he needs each day: "One of them is something to look up to, another is something to look forward to, and another is someone to chase." I was particularly moved by his explanation of the third thing he needs every day:

> My hero. That's who I chase. Now when I was fifteen years old, I had a very important person in my life come to me and say, "Who's your hero?" And I said, "I don't know, I gotta think about that. Give me a couple of weeks." I come back two weeks later, this person comes up and says, "Who's your hero?" I said, "I thought about it. You know who it is? It's me in ten years." So you see, every day, every week, every month, and every year of my life, my hero's always ten years away. I'm never gonna be my hero. I'm not gonna attain that. I know I'm not, and that's just fine with me, because that keeps me with somebody to keep on chasing.

I asked myself out loud, "Who is the version of me ten years from now that I want to chase?" Another voice inside me enthusiastically responded, "You've been wanting to take acting classes for a while. *Do it!*" Suddenly a jolt of electrifying energy ran through my body. I felt myself come *alive*. I immediately searched online for acting classes in Austin, Texas, and found an acting teacher. I was represented by an agent, so I also emailed him and asked where I could take acting classes. In minutes he responded with a few options. And within forty-eight hours, I was signed up for my very first acting class.

Your desires will begin to materialize when you listen and respond to the sparks that make you feel alive in your body. By asking myself that one question out loud, "Who is the version of me ten years from now that I want to chase?" I challenged myself to expand what was possible for me. Because the truth was,

I had wanted to act since I was seven years old and was obsessed with Stephanie Tanner from *Full House*. I even got a golden retriever because she had one! At the age of eight, I felt that spark every time my father followed me around with his camcorder. I could easily memorize the lines of any commercial, movie, or TV show. So of course I felt that spark ignite when I asked myself out loud, "Who is the version of me ten years from now that I want to chase?" My body came alive because the desire had never left me; it was just waiting to be sparked. And that day it was sparked by my being curious with myself, out loud. Asking yourself out loud, "Who is the version of me ten years from now that I want to chase?" and allowing yourself to sit with the question without instantly responding will gradually ease you into opening yourself up to your truest desires.

Notice What Lights You Up

Be receptive and open to inspiration. When you start your day, say out loud, "I am open to feeling sparks all around me!" Setting the tone for your day and being intentional about what you focus on will help you stay open throughout the day. Start paying attention to what comes naturally to you and what lights you up. What can you do for hours? When and where do you feel the most connected to your body? Being in nature, walking, watching a movie, or simply sitting and paying attention to your breathing are some ways in which you might get inspired and feel that spark. And when you do feel that spark, notice it and say out loud, "Ooo, I just felt a spark! I wonder what that's about?" Feel the sensations in your body and respond with what you're experiencing in that moment — for example: "I'm feeling tingly in my stomach, and my heart fluttered. I got excited just now." From there, get even more curious and probe: "Share more about these sensations." Breathe and allow your body to speak to you. Whatever surfaces from your body and into your mind, say it out loud.

What I really want you to focus on is how that spark feels inside you. Where in your body do you notice it? Pay close attention to the spark, because it is the essence of your desire. It is your signal that your desires are communicating with you. When you feel that spark, don't ignore it. Say it out loud.

Get Clear on Your Desires

Desire, unlike need, isn't something that is necessary for your survival. Sure, it would be awesome if you fulfilled your desire to [fill in the blank], but you won't die without it. That's why we tend to be dismissive when a desire does pop up, but don't be. Instead, pay attention to how your desire feels inside your body. When you get a spark, first allow yourself to fully feel the energy of that spark running through you. That is your desire speaking.

Once you feel your desires and the corresponding sensations in your body, I want you to start paying attention to cues and signs everywhere. Notice the things in your life that bring you that same feeling as your desires. When you're in conversation with somebody, pay close attention to the things they say that spark that same sensation inside you. What you're doing here is getting your body used to feeling desire. You're no longer a stranger to your own desires. You're becoming more open to the feelings that your desires produce.

Your next step is to channel those feelings into creating your life. For example, let's say that the feeling your desires bring you is one of pure joy and exhilaration, but you don't know what to do with that feeling and how to bring that energy to life in physical form. That's OK. Here's what I want you to do: You're going to make two lists. The first list is a "Don't Want" list, and the second is a "Want" list.

Most people hesitate to express what they want and don't want, to avoid rocking the boat, inconveniencing others, or being perceived as "picky." I'm training you to get crystal clear on what you want and don't want, so that you can get used to speaking your truth no matter how uncomfortable it may feel. I begin this process with looking at what you don't want, because if you don't give yourself permission to say what you don't want, how will you ever be able to say what you *do* want, out loud? There is power in owning what you don't want. Stop feeling bad for not wanting certain things in your life. You're freeing yourself from things that no longer enhance the quality of your life as you travel the path to who you're becoming. You're taking back the reins of your life and customizing it to suit your personality, needs, and desires.

So let's begin by making your "Don't Want" list. Write down everything in your life that you do *not* want. Things that may feel burdensome, heavy, boring, or exhausting. Don't judge any of these things. Write them out and then, one by one, read each item you wrote out loud. Next, I want you to write down and say out loud what you *want* in your life. Use the table below as an example to guide you as you make your own two lists.

DON'T WANT	WANT
Working a nine-to-five job	Career that gives me freedom
Having a boss	Mentorship and guidance, not someone just telling me what to do
Feeling exhausted every day	Feeling excited to get up every day
People who don't support me	Community of people who lift me up and celebrate me

Pay attention to how you feel in your body as you say out loud the items on your "Don't Want" and "Want" lists. You may find that when you say what you don't want you feel constricted in your body. Or maybe, because you're finally giving yourself permission to say what you want out loud, you feel expansive. You might find that you feel lighter when you just focus on what you want. The intention is to continue noticing how it feels in your body to speak your truth out loud, without any judgment. Think of connecting with your desires this way. Something internal or external will ignite the spark inside you. Your job is to observe it, feel it, connect to it through curiosity, respond to it, and bring it to life.

Returning to the lists above as an example, my process of dialoguing prompted by those lists might land me here: "I don't want to feel exhausted every day, and I acknowledge that I desire something more, and that something more is to wake up energized, excited, and grateful for my life — a feeling of excitement and passion every single morning when I open my eyes." Where does the process of dialoguing with your lists land you? Get clear and speak it out loud.

The next step is to write out some options for actions that would help you bring your desire to life. Again using my example of having the desire to wake up energized and excited about my life, here are some things that I might need to do:

- Have a consistent time to rise and to go to sleep.
- Nourish myself with nutritious food.
- Carve out time to pursue my passion project.
- Create a fun morning music playlist.
- Move my body to get my energy.

Write out your own options and then say each of them out loud. Pay attention to how you feel in your body and notice when you feel a "*Yes!*" Let's say that "carve out time to pursue my passion project" produced a clear "*Yes!*" inside me. Then I would say out loud: "I don't want to feel exhausted every day. I want to wake up energized, excited, and grateful for my life. The decision I need to make is to carve out the time to pursue the things in my life that spark my excitement."

Now, the decision to carve out time for my passion project may feel a bit ambiguous. This is where you get to search online for things that you've been curious about — and try them. Schedule what's important to you in your calendar. Put down a deposit for a class. To stay accountable, let your community of friends and colleagues know that you're open to trying new things. The point here is to ask, listen, decide, and follow through.

> The moment you decide, things unfold faster than you expected and are even better than you can imagine.

Conflicting thoughts like "I desire this but can't have it because…" or "Do I have what it takes to create…?" or "Am I wrong for wanting this?" perpetuate the cycle of indecision. We know that we have this desire inside, yet we fear that we will have to sacrifice something to bring it to life. For a moment, consider that any uneasiness you may be experiencing stems from indecision. Whether it's a relationship that you feel unsure about, a job in which you feel unheard and uninspired, or a friendship that feels one-sided, the power of decision is what will fuel your energy and dissipate your uneasiness.

Remember the example of Allie from *The Notebook*? The reason why she struggled with responding when Noah asked her what she wanted is because she was using only her mind to decide. It wasn't until she spent a few nights with Noah and they reconnected that she started to feel the spark of her desire to be with him. Her body was always saying yes, but her mind, and the voices of her parents and society, led her to believe her desire should be a no. Creation of any kind begins with a desire, and desire lives in the body, not the mind. For that desire to come to life, you must get clear on what it is that you want and then decide to follow through.

Every single time you feel a desire, listen to your body. Where in your body does this desire reside? In your chest? Throat? Stomach? Notice the desire you're experiencing and acknowledge it out loud. By writing it down and saying it out loud, you are creating a safe space to truthfully express what is occurring for you. The following written and spoken reflection exercise will help get everything out of your head and onto paper. You can then use what you've written down to make decisions that are aligned with your desires.

MINI–WRITTEN SAY IT OUT LOUD REFLECTION EXERCISE

1. Write down every area of life where you have desires (for example: health, friendships, finances, career, and romantic partnerships).

2. Ask and answer this question out loud and write down your answers for each category: "What am I desiring in this area of my life?" Don't hold back. Be honest and clear about your desires. For example, if in your financial area you desire the funds to take a solo vacation, you might say, "I desire a solo vacation in a beautiful location by the beach where I can relax, restore, and rejuvenate my soul." Use this as an opportunity to converse with yourself out loud, saying what you would say to a friend: "You've been

> wanting to go on this vacation. Trust your decision.
> You know what's best for you." This is where you get
> to tap into the part of yourself that is understand-
> ing, kind, and encouraging.
>
> 3. Ask yourself out loud, "What's the decision I need
>   to make?" Using the example of taking a vacation,
>   the decision you might need to make is setting aside
>   a travel fund. Or the decision might be to put down
>   a deposit for a trip. Write down your decision and
>   say it out loud to solidify it within yourself.

Remember, no one can decide what's best for you. If up until now you've been handing over the reins of your life to your boss, partner, siblings, parents, and strangers on the internet, it's time to get back in the saddle of your life. You have the power to design a life that you are excited about and proud of.

You can be satisfied and still desire more for your life.

There's nothing wrong with wanting more for your life. You can be in a healthy relationship *and* desire deeper connection. You can be grateful for your job *and* have a desire to start your own business. You can have a roof over your head *and* desire travel and new experiences. You can have a family *and* have desires that are just for you. Both can coexist. You do not need to choose one over the other.

Wanting more does not mean that you're ungrateful for what you have right now. In fact, the decision to want more, when made from a place of "there's something missing in my life," will often create a reality that will perpetuate the feeling of scarcity. Practice being grateful for everything in your life, even the things that you wish weren't your current state of reality. From that place of gratitude, make your decisions.

When you keep your desires inside you, they'll blend into the background of your mind chatter. Speaking your desires and decisions out loud allows you to extract what's in your heart and breathe life into it using the power of your voice. Intentionally choose which thoughts you want to focus on, because the energy of your voice, coupled with your courage to say it out loud, has the power to transform your life.

Consider It Done

Whatever it is you desire, it's time for you to make the decision to want more for yourself. Don't get stuck in the dead-end questioning of "But how is it going to happen?" You don't need to know how. All *you* need to do is decide that you want more. Trust that it will happen. Relax into knowing that if you desire it and decide to pursue it, out loud, *and get out of your own way,* it will happen. It may not happen the way you've planned or expected, but it will happen. Make a decision *to decide.* Your voice will guide you to your next step. Courageously pursuing your dreams and becoming the person you want to be are the greatest adventures of a lifetime.

Congratulate yourself. So far in this book you have done a ton of work — learning how to deeply understand your emotional and psychological world, while also creating new habits of giving a voice to your deepest thoughts and feelings. It's time to unify all of the parts of you and start living your best life — out loud!

SAY IT OUT LOUD EXERCISE

Prompt: Start paying attention to what ignites a spark inside you. Notice what interests you, what piques your curiosity, and what you dream about constantly. A good place to start is your childhood. What did you want to do when you were a kid? When you scroll through YouTube or Instagram, what captures your attention? Observe what makes you come alive inside.

Practice: Create a "Don't Want" and a "Want" list. Write out what you don't want and what you do want. Say out loud everything you wrote down from your "Don't Want" list. Then I want you to say out loud what you want in your life. From there, make a decision based on the desires you've written down and said out loud. When you notice any uneasiness, write down where you feel uneasy, then write down and say, out loud, the actions you would need to take in order to feel more confident in your decisions. The practice of writing and saying it out loud is designed to help you come up with solutions, so simply observe any limiting beliefs and thoughts that try to stop you from bringing your desires to life as you continue moving forward.

Promise: Promise to honor your desires. Anytime you find yourself desiring something and immediately receive a thought that shoots your desire down (for example, "Oh, I can't have that" or "That's silly"), you will honor your desires by saying them out loud to yourself, a trusted friend, or a mentor, and you will hold yourself accountable by making a decision that is aligned with your desires.

SAY IT OUT LOUD AFFIRMATIONS

I can give myself what I need.
I welcome new challenges.
I am letting go of doubt and fear.

Chapter 12

LIVE YOUR LIFE OUT LOUD

Answer this out loud:
What would your life look like if every part of you
felt safe to say it out loud?

When I was four years old, my father would pick me up in his left arm and with great finesse would present me with a paper flower. In his thick Indian accent he would say, "Here's a flower for you." I would almost instantly scrunch my face up, shake my little head from side to side, and say, "No *kundi pee*." *Kundi pee* in my native mother tongue of Tamil is what we know in the United States as "poop." I always had an audience of family members who adoringly laughed at my witty response, but it was clear that anything less than the real thing was unacceptable in my book. I wanted a real flower. No part of me told me to just settle for a paper flower. Quite the opposite.

In my innocence and wholeness, there was no conflict in my mind about my worthiness or being too much. I wasn't afraid of what anyone was going to think of me. I was clear on who I was, and I wasn't afraid to be, feel, or say it. I'm not suggesting that you start saying, "No *kundi pee*" out loud anytime you want to say no to something. Rather, I want you to pay close attention to the parts of you that have settled for anything less than what you really want. Because how often in our adult lives do we accept less than what we are worth? We've been saying "Yes" to accepting "*kundi pee*" much of our lives.

Living your life out loud has nothing to do with how much you talk or the volume you use to speak. It has everything to do with you being crystal clear on what you want and having zero hesitation claiming it out loud. You want to change careers? Awesome! Say it out loud. First to yourself and then to the people you feel safe with. Let them hold you accountable and call you forward in your life. Do you want a loving, passionate, and adventurous romantic relationship? Own it! Say it out loud. Let it be known to your trusted friends and community. You don't have to go through life all alone. Start speaking life into what you want. Don't be afraid to say it out loud. You may run across people who just don't understand you or how you think. Use that as information and ask yourself out loud, "Does this person add value to my life?" Be honest with yourself.

Imagine having the courage to be exactly who you are, without apology — from how you think to how you speak to yourself, from how you interact with strangers to how you dress, from how you treat yourself to how you observe your emotions and respond rather than react. It is a moment-to-moment choice to tune inward, notice the thoughts in your mind, feel the cues of your body, use your voice to guide you, and embody the truth of who you are.

Living your life out loud requires you to feel at home within yourself. Because the truth is, not everyone will understand you. Not everyone will like you. And at the end of the day, you will *always* have you to come home to. Make it a safe place for you to just be every single part of you. You are a multidimensional being. Allow all the parts of you to feel safe to express themselves.

In this final chapter, you will learn how to speak to the part of you that is ashamed of truly being seen, heard, and creatively expressed. This is the part of you that carries around beliefs about being perceived as weird and different. This is also the part of you that is the essence of who you are and, more often than not, the part of you that has been discarded. Learning to speak to this part of you will help you access the power and courage within yourself to live as the fullest expression of yourself, out loud and free of shame. These are the voices in our heads that we need to pay attention to and be able to speak to so that we can face our fears with determination and compassion.

Are You Afraid to Be Your Best Self?

During the time I took an interest in stand-up comedy and acting, I bought Masterclass, the online education platform where I could learn from experts such as Steve Martin, Usher, and Issa Rae. My newfound love of comedy and acting made me hungry to learn everything I could from the best of the best. I immediately became enthralled by how Steve Martin approached the creative process of comedy. When teaching about onstage presence, he asked a question that I hadn't revisited in a while: "Who are you at your best?" That one question threw me off, because I rarely thought of myself as being good at anything, let alone best. I typically strove to do the "right" thing and be good and act like I had it all figured out.

Anytime I would even envision myself at my best, a belittling voice inside would consistently remind me of all my inadequacies. The concept of me at my best was something I rarely focused on. For as long as I could remember, my attention had been toward fixing everything "wrong" with me.

Allowing myself to envision and feel the expanded expression of myself was overwhelming. On the rare occasions I did, I would let my mind freely wander and notice the sensations in my body as a clearer image of the best version of myself gradually came to life. Looking back, I see that one part of me was afraid to get crystal clear on who I wanted to become. Because the minute I got clear on who I wanted to become and what I wanted in my life, I would no longer be able to let myself off the hook with the multitude of excuses I habitually fell back on as to why I couldn't pursue my dreams. I was terrified that I would have no choice but to remove people in my life who were dragging me down. And what if I failed... or what if I ended up succeeding? WOW! Me actually succeeding at something? Would people think I was arrogant? Would I end up all alone because no one would find me relatable?

My body wasn't trained to handle the intensity of sensation and energy that arose during these moments. It was filled with way too much shame to even fathom feeling that intensity of openness and expansion. The thought of feeling that big terrified me. Could I handle that? But the idea of being at my best not only terrified me — it also made me come alive. Asking, "Who are you at your best?" out loud awakened me to the power that I had held all along to create exactly who I wanted to become.

The same goes for you. Picture it already done in your mind. Hold on to the trust and belief that you have everything you need inside you to bring the best you forward.

See It to Be It

When visualizing who you are at your best, find a comfortable position, either seated or lying down; close your eyes; and breathe in and out gently and deeply. Then ask yourself out loud, "Who is [insert your first name] at their best?" Use all your senses, including your intuition, to bring images of your future self and different sensations to the surface. Start speaking out loud what you see and feel. For example: "I feel so free. People are drawn to my energy and my honesty. I am surrounded by friends who understand me, who champion me, who celebrate me. And who love me exactly as I am. I trust that everything is working in my favor. I can see myself writing books, helping people free themselves of shame and live their lives out loud." Continue to say out loud the most specific details of this best version of you — from what you wear, to how you wake up in the morning and get ready for the day, to the kind of food you put into your body.

Notice how you feel in your body as you visualize out loud. You may feel pumped up by seeing your future self clearly! Or it might make you nervous because it feels so close, yet so far away. In those moments, soothe yourself by breathing in and out or by expressing what you're experiencing out loud: "Wow, even saying this out loud is feeling electric in my body. It's something I haven't felt in a long time. It feels uncomfortable, but also something I want to feel more often." Be gentle with yourself — you are allowing a new vision of you to come into your mind and settle into your body. It will take time to get used to it. Every day is an opportunity to unlearn, relearn, and learn something brand-new about yourself and the world around you. With every piece of input you're receiving from your thoughts and the external world, you have the opportunity to pause and ask yourself if that piece of input is bringing you closer to or farther from your best self.

Being the best possible version of yourself requires learning to understand the worst parts of you.

Our family had just landed in the Hyderabad airport. The whiff of cow dung, pollution, and body odor slapped me in the face as soon as we stepped outside the plane. A little girl who couldn't have been more than four or five was carrying what must have been her baby brother. I was a few years older than her. She was barefoot, wearing tattered clothes, and she held out her right palm. I looked her in the eyes and immediately felt like I was the one begging for money. I instantly felt shame, sorrow, and powerlessness. Shame because she was the one begging and I wasn't. Sorrow that she had to live in those conditions. Powerlessness because I didn't know how to make her situation better. I internalized what I perceived as shame and embarrassment and made it my own. On that trip everything that I saw and experienced felt like it was happening to me, like I was the one going through it.

As we get older, traumatizing experiences multiply, and we continue to move through life with unresolved trauma stored in our bodies. Regardless of what you have gone through personally and what you have witnessed, anything that you have not processed stays trapped in your body. These unexpressed parts of us, when kept silent, will express themselves through dis-ease, in both our body and mind.

And that's why it's so hard to visualize ourselves at our best. We still haven't dealt with the worst parts of us — the worst being our pain, judgments, defense mechanisms, addictions, habits, and overall attitude toward ourselves. We've masterfully built our defenses against ever having to deal with the worst parts of us being scrutinized, mocked, teased, and ridiculed, so how could we possibly have a conversation about being at our best? You can't be your best if you're unwilling to sit, understand, and acknowledge the worst parts of you.

The daily practice of saying your thoughts out loud, asking yourself heart-expanding, direct, and open-ended questions, and responding with curiosity and gentle probing will help create internal safety and trust while bringing your vision to life, *easefully*. You won't be in such a rush anymore. You'll trust that the things you desire will unfold according to your divine timing.

Speak to the Worst Parts of You

The parts of ourselves that we are most ashamed of are the very parts that need to be spoken to in order to free us of shame. There are two questions that you can ask anytime you notice a part of you feeling unsafe, scared, or hesitant to express itself: "What is this part of me afraid of more than anything in the world?" and "What does this part of me need to say out loud to free itself?"

Speak to this part of you with the same softness that you would use with a good friend or a child. Each part of us has a purpose. And until we allow it to share what exactly that is, the voice of that part will continue to be driven by fear. What it needs from you is understanding. You will notice that some parts of you are easier to acknowledge than others. Some parts you will be able to connect with quickly by asking a question out loud and responding. With other parts, however, creating trust and open dialogue will take longer. Remember, asking and answering out loud is all about building a safe space for all the parts of you to speak to you and through you!

When you give a voice to the parts of you that feel shame, witness them fully, and love yourself through the process *fully*, that is when you become unshakable. You're no longer shunning parts of yourself; you're learning to embrace them. Do you really think you're going to be concerned with the opinions of others? No. Because *you* have unconditionally accepted yourself.

Ask out loud, "What is this part of me afraid of more than anything in the world?" and respond honestly out loud. Maybe you're afraid that if you become the person you know you can be, you'll end up all alone. Or perhaps you're looking to transition out of your present career into something new, but you feel ashamed to ask for help, so you stay exactly where you are or get so frustrated that you give up.

Once you understand what you're afraid of, then ask yourself, "What does this part of me need to say out loud to free itself?" Right now, your body might feel anxious or scared to speak authentically, and your mind interprets that as it being unsafe for you to live your life out loud. By asking yourself the question "What does this part of me need to say out loud to free itself?" you are integrating your mind, body, and intuition into the conversation. Once you ask and answer this question, I want you to picture how you would feel if you shared this part of yourself out loud. Where would you share that part of yourself and with whom? What would that look like? Picture yourself having said whatever you were holding inside. How do you feel immediately after saying it out loud? As you visualize, say what you are experiencing out loud. Don't hold back. For example: "This is a part of me that I have kept hidden for so long. Saying it out loud and even admitting it to just one person outside of me would make me feel like I can breathe again. I've been holding on to this shame for so long, and all I want is to feel free."

Acknowledge your pain, experience, and feelings. Maybe you've been holding on to a secret that has been eating at you for years. You've harbored immense shame and have been beating yourself up over it. Or maybe you've never allowed yourself to process the pain of a specific event in your life. You tucked it neatly away, and now that part of you is nudging at you to be heard and expressed. Say it out loud. I've had clients share that they were able to walk themselves through painful memories that were repressed. By speaking to those parts of themselves, the suppressed voices inside began to open up and share the depth of their pain, out loud. You are witnessing you in your entirety of human expression — and at the end of the day, isn't that what we seek from others?

When you lean inward, tune in, and allow your inner voice to be heard, you gain access to a wealth of resources. Keep the feeling of who you are at your best at the forefront of your consciousness. You're going to have moments when you want to give up on yourself. Go back to any of the chapters that relate the most to your current situation. Go through the exercises out loud, in front of a mirror, wherever you feel comfortable. Let your energy move through you and out of you in the form of words.

> **Living your life out loud is the embodiment of devotion to all the parts of you.**

Sometimes I think about how my life would have turned out if I had known how to speak to the different parts of me during my teenage years, college days, divorce, mental health struggles, breakups, and addiction. Maybe I wouldn't have gotten to the point of going to rehab, not once, but twice. Maybe I wouldn't have strayed so far from myself that I couldn't even look at myself in the mirror anymore. Maybe I would have cultivated a solid friend group, rather than relying on a toxic relationship to give me company. And let's be real. The maybes are irrelevant at this point. They don't matter. What matters is how I choose to treat myself starting right now.

You're here now, reading this book filled with lessons from all my maybes. How beautiful is that? That's the power of living your life out loud. You begin to inspire others to live their lives out loud. When you start to see everything that has happened *to* you as the most beautiful gift *for* you, you begin to shift how you speak to yourself, treat yourself, and understand yourself. You're no longer in the passenger seat of your life. You're the driver. The whole point of saying it out loud is to be honest with yourself about every single part of you. It's to help you feel free inside, so that anywhere you show up, you show up as fully you. And when you show up as *you*, you inspire other people to show up authentically as themselves. That is the power of saying it out loud and ultimately of living your life out loud. Every single part of you is worthy of being expressed. Things may have happened in your life that made you lose sight of your truth, but you have the power to regain your self-respect.

Living your life out loud is you in your highest and purest form of creation. There will be new chapters, new obstacles, and new lessons ahead. This book offers a foundation of principles that, when applied with openness and curiosity, will transform your triggers into your greatest teachers and your resistance into reverence. Incorporate saying it out loud as a daily practice to cleanse and purify your creative channel. Remember the tools you have learned here; review and practice them every day as you go forward into the world. And if you get stuck, ask yourself this question: "What does this part of me need to say out loud?"

Breathe. Listen. Say it out loud.

SAY IT OUT LOUD AFFIRMATIONS

I am worthy of an extraordinary life filled with fun, play, and ease.

I can be whatever I want to be.

I am not defined by my past; I am fueled by my future.

I cherish my uniqueness, and it is safe for me to live my life out loud.

ACKNOWLEDGMENTS

Writing this book was a group effort. Every single part of me, each with its own unique voice and way of expressing itself, came together to write this book, out loud. *Say It Out Loud* is the integration of every part of me that I have come to know and be in full acceptance of up to this point in time. There are parts of me that I am still discovering and learning about, and as long as I can, by the grace of God, I will continue to say it out loud, to give voice to all the parts of us that still suffer in silence.

Virginia Cummings, my childhood therapist: Thank you for creating a safe space for all the parts of me to say it out loud.

Richelle Fredson: Thank you for going back and forth with me on Facetime when I first wanted to join your book proposal coaching program. And for looking me straight in the eyes and telling me that you believed in me. Your belief set in motion a series of events that I am forever grateful for.

Wendy Sherman: I had my sights set on you years ago and once thought to myself (out loud, of course), "One day she will be my literary agent." I had no idea what my book would be about. All I knew was that you had the type of certainty and tenacity that I was instantly drawn to. Thank you for connecting me with Georgia Hughes at New World Library and being willing to walk through the process of creating this book.

Georgia Hughes: I will never forget that Zoom session where the *Say It Out Loud* book was born. Thank you for creating this book with me. Because of you, your feedback, and the way you guided me throughout this entire process, I healed the part of me that believed I was a terrible writer. For that, I am forever grateful to you.

To the outspoken, powerful, soft-hearted, kind, generous, and brilliant women in my life: Thank you for being my hype women, friends, sisters, and beautiful colleagues. I have learned that it is safe for me to say it out loud with all of you. I have never felt more accepted, safe, and FREE. Our friendships have helped me become honest with myself and express my needs out loud, and for that, I cherish you.

To the strong, kind, and gentle men in my life who are like my brothers: Thank you for being there and serving as a voice of reason for me.

My Say It Out Loud community and clients: The stories that you have shared with me are sacred. My motivation to be more of who I am is due to you. My promise is to keep lighting the way and showing you what is possible when you say it out loud, trust in yourself, and get out of your own way.

Madhu Aunty and Baji Mama: Thank you for always listening to me and making me feel so accepted, seen, and heard, even at a young age. I hope you know how much of an impact you had on my childhood and on who I have become today, all because of your love and acceptance. You will forever be my safe space to be myself, completely as I am.

Pallavi (Akka): Thank you for being the type of sister I can truly #sayitoutloud to no matter how I am feeling. You are the most supportive sister I could ask for, even though you will never stop making fun of how badly I speak Tamil (LOL).

My mother, Geetha, and my father, Shanti: Thank you for giving me the space to figure out who I wanted to become in this lifetime. Both of you were meant to be my parents. I can see that everything between us is exactly how it was divinely ordained to be.

To my late uncle Lakshmi Kumar, who took his life: I wish you had known how to talk to the voices in your head. Maybe then you would still be alive. Your suicide showed me what would happen if I didn't learn how to be kinder to myself. Your death saved my life. I will honor the life that you could have lived by continuing to share your story.

Vachi, my inner child: Thank you for nudging me to shine more brightly, encouraging me to have more fun, and trusting me to protect your heart. Never stop nudging me. You're the reason why I boldly #sayitoutloud. I love you.

ABOUT THE AUTHOR

Vasavi Kumar, a first-generation Indian immigrant, is on a mission to awaken the hearts, minds, and voices of people from all walks of life. She has a fiery passion for empowering those around her to free themselves from the shackles of shame, honor their deepest truth, and say it out loud. She is a licensed therapist and the outspoken host of the *Say It Out Loud with Vasavi* podcast, which inspires, encourages, and teaches people to transform the conversation they're having with themselves internally, so they can spread their beautiful ideas as authentically as possible. She runs the powerful twelve-week Say It Out Loud Safe Haven community for coaches, creatives, and entrepreneurs. Vasavi holds dual master's degrees, one in special education from Hofstra University and one in social work from Columbia University. She is also a trained voice-over artist for audiobook narration and other projects that allow her to use her voice in fun and creative ways. In her free time, she enjoys singing, tennis, traveling, cooking, and spooning with her golden retriever, Laney. She lives in Austin, Texas. Her website is VasaviKumar.com.